WEM-BER-LEE

JOHN McNICOLL

WEM-BER-LEE

The Goal That Kickstarted Sir Alex Ferguson's Manchester United Dynasty

Foreword by Wayne Barton

pitch

First published by Pitch Publishing, 2025
1

Pitch Publishing
9 Donnington Park,
85 Birdham Road,
Chichester, West Sussex,
PO20 7AJ

www.pitchpublishing.co.uk
info@pitchpublishing.co.uk

A CIP catalogue record is available for this book from the British Library.

ISBN 978 1 80150 999 2

Typesetting and origination by Pitch Publishing

MIX
Paper | Supporting responsible forestry
FSC® C010615

Printed and bound on FSC® certified paper in line with our continuing commitment to ethical business practices, sustainability and the environment.

Printed and bound in India by Thomson Press

Contents

Acknowledgements

FIRSTLY, I would like to thank everyone at Pitch Publishing for making this happen. I appreciate everyone's help and input over the last few years as I have plotted my writing journey to where I am now. Thanks to Paul, Jane, Alex, Duncan and anyone else in the background that I may have missed. Thanks to Coxy, Danny Boy, Dicky and Reidy who have listened to me babbling on about writing books for the past few years, even though I know none of you will buy this due to all being anti-Manchester United and I'm cool with that. To Wayne Barton for supplying a foreword that I knew he would be capable of producing and for giving me the platform to start all this in the first place, when I contributed to a couple of his websites back in the day. Thanks to my wife, Kayleigh, who has had to endure the hundreds of hours of me tapping away on my laptop.

And now for everyone who helped contribute, no matter how big or small. Let's start with the man himself, Lee Martin. Lee was very kind enough to give me some of his time to talk about the events and how they unfolded and for that I am truly grateful. Pete Molyneux for sending me match reports and memories of his days following United both home and away. Pete Boyle for his voice notes on his beloved United. David Griffin (Hereford United), Adam Moloney, Jon Bailey, David Leach (Manchester United) and many others that I may have missed out. Thank you all for your comments, snippets and memories on a season that divided so many but ended in the most colourful fashion. 'It's glory and honour,' the great man said. 'There's nothing on earth like being a red.' – Sir Matt Busby

Foreword

WHEN LEE Martin scored the decisive goal in the 1990 FA Cup Final replay, he set the wheels in motion of the most successful managerial reign in English football history. In the context of the time, however, he was the last man in the 1989/90 season who could claim to have saved Alex Ferguson's job as Manchester United manager.

Who are the others? Well, we have Martin Edwards, the chairman of the club, who had the responsibility to determine this. He assured Ferguson that his job would be safe. Mark Robins, who scored at the City Ground to eliminate Nottingham Forest in the third round of the FA Cup. Nigel Jemson, the Forest forward, had boasted before the game he would get Fergie the sack – and had a late goal in the match disallowed. Then, in the fourth round at Hereford United – where defeat would have been more embarrassing than it would have been at Forest – Clayton Blackmore scored late on. Two weeks later, Mark Hughes's goal at a similar point won the league game at Millwall to stop United dropping into the relegation zone. Les Sealey was the goalkeeper Ferguson turned to when he felt keeping faith in Jim Leighton could be fatal to his team's chances. And then, of course, there was the young left-back, Martin. It was a precarious time and, in truth, each of those men did play a significant role.

Given all this, it was an eventful campaign – and that's before mentioning five expensive new recruits, the controversy of a potential takeover, one of the most infamous defeats in the club's history and the death of one of United's most legendary figures. All of these factors combined to create one of the most pivotal seasons in Manchester United history.

United are a club where it is feasible to write a book about every season they've ever played and there would likely to be an illuminating storyline or two in each to entertain us alongside the run of matches and results. But the 1989/90 season is so engaging because of the controversy, the *sliding doors* moments, the 'what ifs' that are presented.

It also feels like a season that acts as a division between the past and the present; the 1990 World Cup, Gazza's tears and all that, seemed to be watched on every English television. Games were being aired on television more frequently, BSkyB came along and, soon after, came the Premier League, where supporters and football fans could now watch a football match or two every single week from the comfort of their armchair. The sport would change forever. Not all of those changes were for the better.

Even for those United supporters who enjoyed every step of the journey that followed, there is a genuine nostalgia associated with the days just before the club scaled the top of the mountain. It could well be a matter of accessibility; where it was still possible to bump into your favourite player on the forecourt of Old Trafford or even watch them train at The Cliff. You could get a photograph or autograph with them. They might even live on your street. Tickets were cheaper. There was none of the disillusion of modern football and its incessant marketing. In fact, it was quite the opposite. The game had an image problem, the supporters were, unfairly, seen as the cause of it as a result of the tragedies at Heysel and then Hillsborough. Those dark days led to the advent of all-seater stadiums, which brought about welcome safety improvements but led to what many felt was a loss of atmosphere.

So, there is a tendency to reminisce, and romanticise, over a time before all that changed. That it is a period of time that neatly coincides with Manchester United's return to prominence provides a small window, between 1989 and 1992, where those of us old enough to remember can recall a moment where the anticipation of those days returning was so exciting and those not old enough can read records such as this in order to be educated and entertained. Yet, it was far from an inevitability. There were days of despair, of genuine instability, of fear that United would have to endure another fresh start. The stakes were high. The jeopardy was real.

This book is a fine chronicle of the 1989/90 season at Old Trafford and it is wonderful to see John, on his fourth book, finally tackle his beloved United by writing about a season that surely means as much to him as it does to any one of us who remember it.

Wayne Barton, September 2024

Introduction: The Beginning of the End?

A PROTEST had never been held inside Old Trafford before and why would it have? This was a place where heroes had been worshipped every other Saturday afternoon since 19 February 1910, when Manchester United moved from their Bank Street stadium to the industrial estate just a stone's throw away from the Manchester Ship Canal. Old Trafford is an iconic stadium in this country, with England and United legend Sir Bobby Charlton once saying 'This is Manchester United football club, this is the theatre of dreams' and, when asked to elaborate on his statement, adding: 'It's here, on this special pitch, where many dreams have come true. It's a place where the cheering of the crowd can turn regular players into legends and where every goal, save and tackle becomes part of football history.'

But despite this footballing utopia, there was trouble brewing and the natives were beyond restless. This was now a call to arms, with swarms of Reds in the stands showing their discontent at what was unfolding in front of their very eyes. Dark clouds were gathering over Trafford Park and that wasn't just the daily Manchester rain, it was something far more sinister. The groans and moans from the terraces had reached an ear-shattering level and it was at this moment that the right to peacefully protest was executed.

On 9 December 1989, Manchester United supporters were at a tipping point. The weather was dire but not as dreadful as the football that was being served up on a weekly basis. Crystal Palace came to Old Trafford that Saturday afternoon having not won a single away game thus far and having recently been put to the sword at Anfield when Liverpool stuck nine past a hapless Eagles defence without reply. Palace were sent back to south London licking their wounds following a 9-0 mauling in a game that consisted of nine different goalscorers.

The writing looked to be on the wall again for the visitors when Russell Beardsmore opened the scoring after just nine minutes but what then followed was a bundle of missed chances from the home side, who were unable to capitalise on their slender lead. Then, just before half-time, Mark Bright equalised for the London club before adding a second ten minutes after the restart. It was at this moment that the fans began their demonstration … well, one in particular. Pete Molyneux was a United diehard who had followed his idols, both home and away, for three decades. This turgid display in front of Old Trafford's lowest crowd of the season prompted 'Molly' to stand on his seat and begin his outpouring of emotion.

'Anyone who knows me would tell you I'm United through and through. I never slag off the team, even after bad performances,' he said. 'I always see the glass half full. Loyalty to United is in my DNA. When I decided to call for Fergie's head, I knew exactly what I was doing. I fully understood that the scale and intensity of the protest could leave the manager severely embarrassed, possibly humiliated. I didn't take the decision lightly; it was the culmination of several months' frustrations.'

His words were presented to Ferguson on a banner that Molyneux had made himself on a bedsheet, using black paint. It read: '3 Years of Excuses – And It's Still Crap … Ta Ra Fergie.' In fact, the banner was a few weeks in the making, as 'Molly' had planned to unfurl it a month earlier on Ferguson's three-year anniversary in early November. 'We were playing Forest but there was a minute's silence for Remembrance Sunday, so it didn't feel right and I kept it in a plastic bag by my feet,' recalled Molyneux. 'The next game was Chelsea and I didn't want to do it against one of our serious rivals. But Palace came after that and it was a dreadful performance and a dreadful day. We took the lead but then Mark Bright scored twice and I thought "Right, this is the right moment".'

Pete had seen enough and it was at this point that he was acting like a jilted lover, trying to regain the attention of his ex, with his focus on venting his frustrations and anger solely towards the manager. 'I was shaking,' said Molyneux. 'I loved the club and I was apprehensive people would turn on me but the reaction was amazing. It was like a domino effect around the ground as people realised what the banner said, culminating in this crescendo of cheers and applause.' It was a bold move but one that was clearly needed to shed light on how the match-going fans felt at that time.

'Of course, I never expected United's board to sack Fergie just on my say so,' said Molyneux. 'I simply wanted to get my frustration off my chest and put the strength of our dissatisfaction firmly on the agenda. In that respect, the protest had the desired effect. It also served the purpose of polarising the views of anyone with a mild interest in Manchester United. It ended the covert rumblings amongst supporters and put the debate into the public domain. For the first time in living memory, there had been a mass upsurge against the manager of Manchester United and you either agreed with it or not. The protest provided a platform for supporters to voice their opinion.'

But there had been grumblings amongst supporters prior to this public display. It was a sentiment that had been echoed in the national papers a year earlier, with a Mr Brian Marriot from Cambridge winning the £10 star letter of the week in Jimmy Greaves's column. A furious Mr Marriot wrote: 'Fergie must go. The time has come for Manchester United to sack Alex Ferguson. He's been in charge for more than a year and has spent £2m on new players. Yet the team now is even worse than the one he inherited from Ron Atkinson. United will never win anything while he's the manager.'

Now, with the fanbase of the Red Devils seemingly on the turn, it was the match-going supporters who were making their feelings clear to the boss, who was stood on the sideline watching his team succumb to yet another defeat, their second at Old Trafford and seventh of the season just shy of the festive period. The final whistle blew and a small portion of travelling Palace fans rejoiced that their team had picked up their first three points on the road that season. United fans, on the other hand, jeered and booed the boys in red off the field, with many a word in anger aimed at the manager as he swiftly headed off down the tunnel. The atmosphere around the club was turning toxic. Surely it was only a matter of time before the boss was relieved of his duties.

Just seven days later and Ferguson was again subjected to a crescendo of whistles and abuse as United crashed to a second consecutive home defeat, this time at the hands of Tottenham Hotspur. Gary Lineker fired Spurs into the lead to further intensify the pressure on the under-fire boss, who by now must have been wondering how he was going to dig himself out of this hole. Performances were getting worse, as well as the numbers coming through the turnstiles at Old Trafford and who could blame them? There was no glimmer of light peeking through the clouds, certainly not over M16.

A 0-0 draw against Queens Park Rangers on New Year's Day at Old Trafford had the manager's job hanging by a thread, with reports that a chat between Michael Knighton (more on him later) and club chairman Martin Edwards had taken place post-match, with Edwards apparently saying: 'We need to discuss the manager.' It was a situation that was seemingly spiralling out of control for the board, who were desperate to back their man but, at the same time, were starting to feel the heat from fan power as the club surrendered yet another chance of a league title at the halfway stage of the campaign.

But how did we get to here?

Genesis of a Football Club

MANCHESTER UNITED had become a national icon, with their fame beginning to spread further across the globe. It wasn't just a football team on an industrial estate in Trafford Park anymore. We were now beginning to see the start of a boom period, although the creation of the Premier League and all its riches were still a few years away. For a club of this size, with its fantastic support and infrastructure, the thought of another blank in the title wins column was a massive concern from everyone associated with the Red Devils. It was a long and eventful process to get to this stage, with several bumps along the road, but many had felt that the club were somewhat stuttering and fluffing their lines at present.

The very beginning saw the club's formation in 1878 as Newton Heath LYR Football Club but it was nearly a decade later that the club would play in its first ever competitive match, an FA Cup tie in 1886. Fast forward another two seasons and, in what you would call the club's first meaningful campaign, they finished eighth in the Football Alliance league. It wouldn't take long for the club to start to build and in 1892, it applied for entry to the Football League. However, they found it tough going and were relegated to Division Two in 1894.

It was a tough pill to swallow and Newton Heath were barely treading water in the division as they looked for a return to the top flight. In doing so, the club was starting to struggle behind the scenes. In 1902, the club faced financial turmoil and was on the brink of extinction. A local brewer named John Henry Davies stepped in and rescued the team, renaming it Manchester United. Under Davies's ownership, the club began to stabilise, eventually gaining promotion back to the top division in 1906 and two years later, they won their first major trophy by lifting the First Division title.

Legend has it that John Henry Davies stumbled into becoming a club owner with his takeover of Newton Heath. According to the story, the club captain Harry Stafford's dog (a St Bernard named Major) wandered away from the player at the club fundraising bazaar at St James's Hall, Manchester, in February 1901. Major was found by Davies, who returned him to Stafford. Davies asked if he could buy the dog but instead ended up donating to the club. As a gesture of thanks, Stafford allowed him to keep the dog. In March 1902, at a meeting at the New Islington Hall, Stafford announced to Newton Heath supporters that he, Davies and three other local businessmen had agreed to invest £200 each in the club in order to save it after a winding-up order had been issued two months earlier.

One of Davies's earliest moves was to change the colours of the team to red and white, as well as installing Ernest Mangnall as the manager. He not only oversaw the championship triumph in 1908 but also claimed the inaugural Charity Shield, held between United and Queens Park Rangers. It took a replay for the two sides to be separated but overcome Rangers they did. The following season saw the team's league form dip drastically but the club claimed its first-ever FA Cup win, defeating Bristol City 1-0 in the final.

Two years later, in 1911, and United and Mangnall were top of the pops again. This time, however, the club were competing in new surroundings, with Davies securing a deal to play at Old Trafford, with United leaving their old Bank Street stadium in 1910. It was a bold move but one that the owner gambled on at a time when attendances were rapidly increasing, as was the popularity of the sport in general. For Mangnall, though, this was the end of the road as far as he was concerned – he was hotfooting it across town to take up the manager's position at Manchester City.

Following his departure, the team began to falter in the league and neither T.J. Wallworth nor John Bentley could change the fortunes of the club in the period leading up to the outbreak of World War One. Jack

Robson took the reins between 1914 and 1921 but his tenure was blighted by the outbreak of war and his team was decimated by players not returning from serving for their country. John Chapman replaced Robson but was unable to stop the club tumbling into Division Two in 1922 and it would only be at the third time of asking that Chapman would eventually lead United back into the top tier.

His first attempt at the First Division in 1925/26 brought a ninth-place finish but a poor start to the following campaign saw Chapman relieved of his duties in October 1926. His replacement was Clarence Hilditch. Chapman had, in fact, received a telegram from the Football Association suspending him from all football activities. 'Lal' Hilditch was one of the Manchester United players at the time, so this was arguably one of the earliest instances of a player-manager at a top club. Hilditch managed to steady the ship but was replaced at the end of the season by Herbert Bamlett. Bamlett's stint was less than spectacular and after three seasons, including a relegation back to Division Two, he parted ways with the club.

John Henry Davies passed away in 1927, leaving the club in a better place than when he founded it but the finances were looking precarious following the war and with the country affected by the Great Depression. James W. Gibson acquired the club in 1931 and immediately injected around £40,000 to help with the running costs and pay off the surplus debt. The club were in Division Two and looked to the services of club secretary Walter Crickmer, who took on the manager's role in 1931. After a single season under Crickmer, Scott Duncan was charged with lifting the club back into Division One. It was a challenge that Duncan accepted and then excelled at, as he not only gained promotion in 1935/36 but won the Second Division title in the process. Unfortunately for Duncan, what goes up must come down and in this case it was United as the Red Devils crashed straight back through the relegation trapdoor.

Despite fleeting success, Duncan's time at Old Trafford was up and Crickmer was again called upon to lead the team. What Crickmer or anyone else didn't know at the time was that we were less than two years away from World War Two. Crickmer stayed at the helm until the war had ended in 1945, albeit that there had been little to no football played during that period, with players serving their countries both home and away. In 1941, tragedy struck at Old Trafford when the club's stadium was severely damaged during a German air raid. Crickmer was believed to be one of the first on the scene, as he was working as a special police constable during the war, but could only stand and watch his beloved stadium burn and crumble.

The rebuilding process was arduous but the spirit of the club remained unbroken. Manchester United had been on the brink of financial ruin, as well as having their home flattened to debris, but they kept on going. It felt like United had hit rock bottom but little did anyone know at the time that the club was still to face its darkest hour. Games would have to be played across town at Maine Road for the foreseeable while construction began to bring the stadium back to a state of good health.

In early 1945, arguably one of the most important pieces of business that the club ever did was to hire a fella by the name of Matt Busby. Busby had plied his trade as a footballer, representing both Manchester City and Liverpool, but his career at Anfield was cut short when World War Two began. Busby was called up for National Service and it was during this time that he served as a football coach in the Army Physical Training Corps, gaining experience and forming opinions on how the beautiful game should be played.

Liverpool offered Busby the chance to join their manager, George Kay, on his coaching staff but, after a meeting with the board, Busby decided that his future lay elsewhere. It was reported that Busby's ideologies were not aligned with those of the men who were courting his services. News in football travels fast and, learning that Busby had rejected Liverpool's approach, Manchester United made their move.

Louis Rocca, an ice cream seller from Newton Heath, had been around the football club for the best part of 30 years. He had been a friend of John Henry

Davies, carrying out various roles at the club and was even assistant to Walter Crickmer at one point. But most important was his ability to convince James W. Gibson to inject some much-needed investment into the club and then the cherry on the cake for United's 'fixer' was a letter that he wrote to his friend, Busby. It was addressed to his army regiment and outlined a position as the manager of Manchester United. As a result, a meeting with Gibson was arranged and, in February 1945, Busby signed on the dotted line and a new dawn at United had begun.

Busby's first task was to hire a man called Jimmy Murphy. Murphy had impressed Busby in a coaching session held between a team of non-commissioned officers and it was at this point that Busby had seen the way in which Murphy had handled not only himself but also the lads he was leading in the session. 'He had us all transfixed,' said Busby. 'It was as if he had put everybody in a footballing trance. I visualised how good he could be for Manchester United.' With a firm handshake cementing the pair's agreement, Murphy joined Busby as his chief coach.

The duo hit it off immediately, mixing a blend of youth and experience amongst the squad. Busby later admitted: 'Jimmy was my first signing and my most important.' Crickmer had spent years previously building the foundations of what would now be classed as a youth set-up by scouting for young, local talent and harvesting them for the first team. This was music to the ears of both Busby and Murphy, whose philosophy was 'if you are good enough, you are old enough'. Murphy picked up the baton from Crickmer and, with the help of coach Bert Whalley, took it to a whole new level. He brought in youth friendlies, reserve friendlies and even tours to Ireland to aid with the search for fresh new talent.

Murphy and Busby were similar in how they perceived the game should be played and it was the pair's footballing knowledge that led to the team's DNA that you see right up to the modern day. Murphy had a set of footballing principles that he looked for when scouting and signing players. A goalkeeper must be confident in his ability and excel at handling. His full-backs (a new trend at the time) would possess both speed and balance, with a key responsibility of overlapping their winger to join in with attacks. He noted that, whilst tackling was still important for a full-back, it wasn't the most important skill required for the role. Murphy's thinking was that, with his full backs marauding down the wings, the opposition team's wingers would spend more time marking them than attacking themselves.

Murphy wanted his central defenders to be tall, athletic, and good readers of the game. They needed to be strong, so as not to be bullied by the opposition frontmen. His midfield was the engine room, with Murphy liking his two central midfielders to operate in different ways. One player would be the 'sweeper', screening the defence and making interceptions to break up the opposition's attacks, while the other would play further forward, linking the play to the forwards. Think Roy Keane and Paul Scholes between 1999 and 2001 when the pair were at their peak playing together. Despite the roles differing slightly, the principles stayed the same, with the players having to be mobile, possess great stamina and a passion for looking after the football. He was a real stickler for passing stats, boasting that a player in that role should give away no more than one pass every five or six attempts.

Then you have your frontmen. Murphy liked to set his teams up with two centre-forwards, with one being at least 6ft tall so that he could pose a dominant aerial threat. They would need to have great stamina, as there was no such thing as a lost cause, with both players having to chase balls in the channels, as well as putting pressure on the opposition defence when they had possession of the ball. And, finally, you had your wingers. These were what Murphy would describe as your game changers. They would need to be lightning quick, show courage on the ball and have unnerving accuracy when delivering crosses into the box. His wingers were also tasked with being able to run back towards their own goal when the team didn't have the ball, so stamina and workrate were a must.

In his first two seasons, Busby – aided by Murphy – guided the team to two consecutive runner-up spots, as well as an FA Cup trophy in 1948. In fact, United finished second in four of the first five seasons Busby was at the helm. It was a marked improvement for a club that had been yo-yoing between the divisions over the previous decade but still they were not quite at the top of the pile. That was until the 1951/52 season when, finally, Busby and Murphy were able to enjoy the fruits of their labours. It was the first top division title win for just over 40 years, although this did include the war years. The club were, once again, the champions of England.

Tragedy and Triumph

ACCOMPLISHED SPORTS authors Charlie Jones and Kim Doren wrote a book back in 2012 titled *If winning were easy, everyone would do it.* The publication looked at how sports stars and teams from years gone by had thrived in their respective fields but showed just what it took to get them to the very top. Of course getting there is one thing but staying there, now that's where the difficulty lies and that was something that Busby and his team were soon to find out.

Having won the charity shield, the team struggled to hit the heights of the previous campaign and could only muster an eighth place finish. Busby could see that some of his squad was aging and it was beginning to show in their performances with the likes of captain Johnny Carey showing no signs of rolling back the years. It was time to start putting his trust in the youth with some of the players brought into the squad as young as 16.

United again fell short of the top with fourth and fifth positions in the league during the 1953/54 and

1954/55 campaigns but the team was beginning to gel and in 1956, the 'Busby Babes' brought home their first title and United's fourth First Division championship. A 2-1 win over Blackpool at Old Trafford had Edgar Turner of the *Daily Mail* waxing lyrical about the match he had just covered. 'This side could be the greatest' was the headline. Turner followed it in with a similar tone. 'What a match to decide a league championship! What a blinder! What a bloody scene in the dressing rooms afterwards!' I think it's clear to see that Turner enjoyed his afternoon's work that day.

The team were nicknamed the 'Babes' but despite their tender age, boy, could they play football. Bill Foulkes, Mark Jones, Jackie Blanchflower (brother of Danny), Albert Scanlon, David Pegg, Billy Whelan and Duncan Edwards were the new heroes worshipped on a Saturday afternoon. Edwards had become the youngest player at that time to be capped by England, at just 17, and was a fantastic footballer who could play in a number of positions on the field, making him a coach's dream.

Having claimed the domestic title in 1956, United had the possibility of competing in a brand new European competition, the European Cup. It was an event that comprised the winners from the continent's domestic leagues and was played in a two-legged knockout format. Chelsea had been denied entry to the inaugural tournament, with Football League secretary

Alan Hardaker refusing to allow the Blues to enter, stating that it could disrupt the integrity of the domestic league. Busby lobbied for United to be granted access and when he took the proposition to a higher body, Stanley Rous at the FA granted United and Busby their wish.

On 27 September 1956, Manchester United and Busby embarked on their first-ever European adventure. Anderlecht were their opponents and United won the first leg in Brussels 2-0. When the Belgian club came to Manchester for the return, the game had to be played at Maine Road due to Old Trafford not having floodlights for the match. Our neighbours from across the way had been very accommodating towards the club, as they had when Old Trafford was being rebuilt following bomb damage. Despite holding an advantage from the first leg, the thought of having to play the home leg at a neutral venue made Busby feel uneasy. 'We were all keyed up for the return match and also a little anxious because we, too, were playing away from home,' he said. Busby needn't have worried, as United stuck ten past the visitors without reply in what the manager described as 'the finest exhibition of teamwork I had ever seen from any side, either at club or international level'. Even having the added workload of the club's new European journey, this never stopped Busby and his charges from challenging for a domestic clean sweep. The Charity Shield was won at the beginning of the campaign and by the end of the 1956/57 season, United were champions of England once again. United captain Roger Byrne said on lifting the trophy: 'Although the league title is the least glamorous of the three, it is the most arduous. Our ambition now is to win it three years on the run like Huddersfield and Arsenal.'

A 5-3 aggregate defeat to Real Madrid put paid to the Red Devils' European dreams but it had been a journey into the unknown and one that the boss had relished. They had fallen short on this occasion but would be back for another shot at Europe's elite the following year. Busby not only wanted to have the best team in the land, he also wanted to have the best team in Europe.

With dreams of a Treble having disappeared, it left just the FA Cup Final, with Aston Villa standing between United and a domestic Double. United were heavy favourites to lift the cup but disaster struck inside six minutes when Peter McParland smashed into United goalkeeper Ray Wood, injuring United's custodian and putting him out of the game. Wood, who suffered a broken cheekbone, would later return to the pitch as an outfield player to help United fill their quota of 11 men. Perpetrator McParland scored twice and Jackie Blanchflower in United's goal was powerless to stop him. A 2-1 defeat meant that Busby would only have the First Division title to show for all his efforts.

Another 'Babe' had been brought into the side that year to add to the growing collection of adolescents.

Bobby Charlton, a midfielder who could also play as a forward, had represented England Schoolboys and signed for United at the age of 15. In October 1956, Charlton made his debut against Charlton Athletic, netting a brace in a 4-2 win over the Addicks. Busby had another gem on his hands and, with the likes of Taylor, Whelan, Viollet and Edwards, the team boasted some serious firepower and had players who had many years of football ahead of them.

Busby and his charges embarked on another European Cup adventure in 1957/58, hoping to go that one step further and make the final. The domestic campaign got off to a solid, if not spectacular, start. The team were playing well in the league and all seemed rosy in the Old Trafford garden. United were trailing Wolverhampton Wanderers by three points at the top of the table but there was still a third of the season remaining – plenty of time to overturn the deficit, so no need to press the panic button just yet.

The team were going full throttle in both cup competitions as well, with the third and fourth rounds of the FA Cup successfully navigated as they beat Workington and Ipswich Town respectively. Shamrock Rovers, Dukla Prague and Red Star Belgrade were dispatched in the European Cup, lining up a semi-final against Italian giants AC Milan. There was still so much to play for and Busby had his team purring just at the right time for what was going to be an exciting run-in to the season. But those lads didn't even get the chance to finish what they had started – well, not all of them.

The date of 6 February will forever be circled on the calendars of everyone connected with Manchester United. On that day in 1958, the darkest day in United's history, 23 people – including eight players and three members of the club's staff – suffered fatal injuries in the Munich air crash. Having drawn the quarter-final second leg in Belgrade 3-3 to complete a 5-4 aggregate victory, United were jubilant after progressing yet again on European soil. The next day, Manchester United team members, as well as journalists and others, boarded a plane to take them first to Munich, for refuelling, and then back to Manchester. Europe was in the grip of winter and by the time they reached Germany, conditions were appalling.

After two aborted take-offs in near-blizzard conditions at Munich-Riem Airport, a third attempt was made. However, the plane was unable to achieve enough speed for take-off and, instead, slid off the end of the runway. After breaking through a fence, the aircraft struck a home and then a shed that contained fuel, causing an explosion. Of the 44 passengers on board that flight, 23 lost their lives, eight of them players. Roger Byrne (28), Eddie Colman (21), Mark Jones (24), David Pegg (22), Tommy Taylor (26), Geoff Bent (25), Liam Whelan (22) and Duncan Edwards (21) were killed, along with club secretary Walter Crickmer ('Mr Manchester United'), trainer Tom Curry and coach Bert Whalley.

Eight journalists also died – Alf Clarke, Tom Jackson, Don Davies, George Fellows, Archie Ledbrook, Eric Thompson, Henry Rose and Frank Swift, who was a former Manchester City and England goalkeeper. The plane's captain, Ken Rayment, perished, as did Sir Matt's friend, Willie Satinoff. Travel agent Bela Miklos and crew member Tom Cable were also among the deceased. As the wreckage of the plane lay burning on the ground, goalkeeper Harry Gregg gathered himself following the accident before setting about a one-man rescue mission. He entered the debris to help pull clear his team-mates and his manager.

Bobby Charlton, Jackie Blanchflower, Dennis Viollet and Matt Busby were all dragged from the scene and brought to safety. It was a real show of heroism and future United star George Best would later say of Gregg's heroics: 'Bravery is one thing but what Harry did was about more than bravery. It was about goodness.' The disaster was an absolute tragedy for the club, who had lost, in the blink of an eye, nearly its entire team. Manchester United's heart had been ripped out. The football world was in mourning.

Peter Howard, a travelling press photographer for the *Daily Mail*, was one of the lucky ones who survived the accident. 'It was snowing when we landed in Munich,' he said. 'We went off for refreshments and then back to the aircraft to continue the flight. I was sitting in the front row of seats on the starboard side. When the pilot tried to take off, there seemed to be some kind of slight fault with the engines. He stopped. Then he tried a second take-off. That did not seem satisfactory, so he taxied back to get things checked up. It was on the third take-off that we crashed. I think we were at the end of the runway, only a bit above the ground.

'The plane suddenly appeared to be breaking up. Seats started to crumble, everything seemed to be falling to pieces. It was a rolling sensation and all sorts of stuff started coming down on top of us. There wasn't time to think. No one cried out, no one spoke … just a deadly silence for what could only have been seconds. I can't remember if there was a bang or not. Everything stopped at once. I was so dazed, I just scrambled about. Then I found a hole in the wreckage and crawled out on my hands and knees.' Unfortunately for some of the others, they weren't so lucky. God rest their souls. RIP.

Now, for eagle-eyed readers, you might have noticed that Jimmy Murphy's name was missing from the manifest of that fatal plane journey. There is a pretty good reason for that. As well as being Busby's assistant, Murphy also held the position of Wales national manager. Leading up to that week, Murphy had been told that his Wales side would need to play Israel in a World Cup qualifying play-off that was to be held on the same day United would face Red Star Belgrade. Murphy was adamant that he would travel with his friend, Busby, and the team but the manager was having none of it and insisted that he go and achieve qualification with his home nation and that Bert Whalley would take his place on the trip.

Murphy arrived back at Old Trafford on Thursday, 6 February 1958 in jovial mood following both Wales' 2-0 win and United's 3-3 draw that led to the team's march into the semi-final of the European Cup. Life was good, really good. And to top it off, Wolverhampton Wanderers were up next for United in a game that Murphy was licking his lips at the prospect of. Wayne Barton, writer of Jimmy Murphy – The Man Who Kept the Red Flag Flying, captured the moment beautifully and poignantly. Murphy had returned to Old Trafford by taxi that day. In that book, Barton wrote:

'Looks like we might win the European Cup this year, Mr Murphy,' the driver said. Jimmy nodded politely and smiled. He was eager to get back to work.

'I got to the office and went past Alma George, who was our secretary then … there seemed to be nobody there. The boss wasn't there, it was strange,' Jimmy recalled. 'No one around at all. I had a drink and gave Alma a drink. She said "Haven't you heard, Jimmy?" I said "Heard about what?" "The plane has crashed".

'"It never struck me at all. She said it again. I had another drink. I took that second one quickly. She said it again and she started to cry. And then it struck me very vividly. I thought "God, no" ... the last thing I would have ever thought of was a plane crash. I went into my office and cried for about 20 minutes. I couldn't realise it. Half of those players you'd brought up, more or less lived with ... it was very difficult.'

The following day, Murphy boarded a plane. His close friend and boss, Busby, was laid in an oxygen tent fighting for his life. But, despite being read the last rites, he was, in true Manchester United style, clinging on for the arrival of Murphy. 'Keep the flag flying, Jimmy,' Busby said in muffled voice, fighting to both speak and breathe. 'Keep things going until I get back.'

Murphy then moved round to the bedside of Duncan Edwards; some would say a favourite of Murphy. 'Oh, it's you, Jimmy,' said Edwards as he struggled to open his eyes. 'What time is kick-off on Saturday? Is it three o'clock? 'Okay, son ... don't worry. We're resting you, Duncan. We don't need you to beat Wolves.' Edwards closed his eyes and murmured: 'Get stuck in.'

Edwards would never make it out of that hospital, passing away a couple of weeks later. 'When I used to hear Muhammad Ali proclaim to the world that he was the greatest, I used to smile,' said Murphy. 'You see, the greatest of them all was an English footballer named Duncan Edwards. If I shut my eyes now, I can see him. Those pants hitched up, the wild leaps of boyish enthusiasm as he came running out of the tunnel, the tremendous power of his tackle, always fair but fearsome, the immense power on the ball. The number of times he was robbed of the ball once he had it at his feet could be counted on one hand. He was a players' player. The greatest … there was only one and that was Duncan Edwards.'

Murphy left that Munich hospital in typically bullish mood. 'As my mind dwelt on the full appalling horror of it all, I thought I would go mad, although I was doing my best to think about the future,' Murphy wrote in his autobiography. 'The Red Devils will rise again,' he told reporters. 'It will be a long, tiring job to rebuild the Red Devils. This time, we'll have to start practically from scratch. But we'll do it. This I do know – United was and, will again, be a great club. We have the greatest club spirit in the world.'

On 19 February, just 13 days after the crash, United faced Sheffield Wednesday in the fifth round of the FA Cup. Only Harry Gregg and Bill Foulkes were available from the team who had faced Red Star Belgrade, forcing Murphy to beg, borrow and steal in order to fulfil the fixture. Derek Lewin, Bob Hardisty and Warren Bradley were transferred to United on short-term contracts by non-league club Bishop Auckland. Bradley was the only one of the three players to play for the first team and the only one to sign a permanent contract. The remaining places in the team were filled by reserve players, including Shay

Brennan and Mark Pearson. Even United's fierce rivals Liverpool offered them five loan players to help put a side together.

The matchday programme for that fixture had been printed with 11 blank spaces for the United team and when Murphy came to fill them in on the day of the game, he broke down in tears. Somehow, riding on the crest of a wave of pure emotion, United won the game 3-0 to advance to the next round of the competition with goals from Alex Dawson and a brace by Shay Brennan. It was this spirit that Murphy had alluded to. In the league, though, finding wins was becoming a different story as the squad that Murphy had left at his disposal was not quite up to the required standard of that of a Manchester United team. But these were the cards that both the club and Murphy had been dealt. There was no sulking, just head down and hard work.

United would only win one more league game for the remainder of that 1957/58 season, a 2-1 victory over Sunderland at Roker Park. With their league form in tatters and an expected exit from the European Cup against Milan, United slumped to a ninth-place finish but somehow, against all the odds, the team reached the FA Cup Final. Following that moving win over Sheffield Wednesday in round five, Murphy guided the Red Devils to wins over West Bromwich Albion and Fulham (both after replays) before facing Bolton Wanderers in the final.

Two goals from Nat Lofthouse put paid to a fairytale ending to the season for United as Bolton ran out two-goal winners but maybe, just maybe, getting to the final in the first place was part of the magic. Lofthouse's second goal was a controversial effort, with Harry Gregg being bundled into the net and receiving treatment for his injury before continuing the match. It was widely considered that it was after this game that referees' rulings on the charging of goalkeepers began to change. Gregg and even Lofthouse himself admitted that the goal should not have stood. Another final and another goalkeeper handicapped in order for the opposition to claim the win. For some, victory was by any means necessary but that wasn't the Manchester United way.

While United's players headed off for their summer break ready to refresh and put this horror of a campaign behind them, Murphy was already putting the wheels in motion for the 1958/59 season and the return of Matt Busby. Albert Quixall was added to the side while Bobby Charlton, whose speedy recovery from his injuries even allowed him to make his England debut within weeks of the Munich disaster, weighed in with 29 goals to fire United to a remarkable second-place finish behind Wolves. It was like Busby and Murphy had sprinkled some magic dust over the players, so impressive were their performances before eventually coming up just short of the title. It was a huge improvement on ninth but it was still a long way short of where the two men in the dugout wanted United to be.

With the team somehow making that FA Cup Final just months after the disaster and then looking like they had never been away in the league the following year, the team eventually seemed to just run out of steam as the wave crashed back down to earth. The following three seasons between 1959/60 and 1961/62 saw two seventh-place and one 15th-place finish in the First Division table. Some of the older heads in the team were now really beginning to show their age and Busby, having made an assessment on what was needed, moved quickly to secure the signature of Denis Law from Torino for a British record fee of around £115,000.

Law made an immediate impact on his debut, scoring after just seven minutes in a 2-2 draw with West Bromwich Albion and went on to finish the campaign as the club's top scorer with 29 goals in all competitions in what was another season of inconsistency in the league. United, in fact, only stayed in the division by the skin of their teeth but they did manage a run of form in the FA Cup, reaching the final, where they would face Leicester City. David Herd struck a brace and Law completed the scoring to secure the 1963 FA Cup with a 3-1 win.

After the game, an elated Busby said: 'I had a few qualms for about five or ten minutes in the second half, when Leicester were fighting furiously to wipe out our lead, but otherwise I was quite contented.' Law had found the match a lot tougher than he anticipated but was in jovial mood as he sat with his winner's medal in his hand. 'The lads played exceptionally well but, although it may have looked easy, I personally found it harder than I expected.' The players in red paraded the trophy on the Wembley pitch as the supporters in red and white spun their scarfs and waved at their heroes.

Behind the scenes, a young player had been spotted in Belfast by scout Bob Bishop and was brought over to Manchester. His name was George Best. Bishop had been in Northern Ireland looking for new talent and once he had set his eyes on this lad with the jet black hair, he knew that his journey had not been wasted. Bishop sent a telegram back to Busby simply saying: 'I think I've found you a genius.' This scrawny kid was brought over and quickly impressed his new potential employers, including Murphy and Busby. He joined United at the age of just 15 and it wasn't all plain sailing with the admin side of the deal. Northern Irish players were unable to join English clubs as apprentices at that time, so they had to find more creative ways of getting him on the payroll.

The new season's curtain-raiser saw United face league winners Everton in the Charity Shield at Goodison Park. It was a horror of a performance from Busby's men as the Toffees ran out 4-0 victors on home soil. It was feared that United's league form from the previous season, which had seen them just one more defeat away from relegation, was still lingering in the team. However, a draw and three wins kickstarted the 1963/64 campaign, which was a pleasant surprise considering the showing in the Charity Shield, and Denis Law picked up where he left off the previous season, showing a keen eye for goal with seven goals in his opening four matches, including a hat-trick in a 7-2 thrashing of Ipswich Town at Portman Road.

That autumn of 1963, Busby decided to give the now-17-year-old lad from Belfast his first-team debut in a home game against West Bromwich Albion. The game, won 1-0 courtesy of a David Sadler goal, gave Old Trafford a tiny glimpse of its latest footballing prodigy. 'Busby crucially learned two things about Best that he had suspected but could not confirm before sending him out against Albion,' writes Best biographer Duncan Hamilton in *Immortal*. 'The grand occasion galvanised rather than diminished him; and his airy attitude was not a fake front designed to disguise self-doubt. Best passed his test. He had taken on Williams, who looked perfectly capable of dicing him into quarters. He'd run at him and taken the ball beyond him. He'd made him lunge and curse. And he'd survived the sort of challenges that would have forced the faint or tender-hearted into instant surrender.'

Despite the anticipation surrounding the youngster, Best would have to wait until the festive period before being rewarded with his second appearance for the club after spending several months impressing in the reserve team, with Busby reportedly ensuring that 'fierce, sometimes brutal' training sessions left Best well used to coping with tough challenges and other rough-house tactics. In just his second start, Best fired home a goal in a 5-1 win over Burnley to give the home fans a taste of what was about to come. In January 1964, Law, Best and Charlton lined up for the first time in a 4-1 demolition of West Bromwich Albion and the United 'Holy Trinity' was born.

Law continued to fire in goals, left, right and centre. The Scottish forward had claimed three match balls, scoring trebles against Ipswich Town and Tottenham Hotspur and even having the audacity to score four against Stoke City. Law ended the 1963/64 season with 46 goals in all competitions but it wasn't enough to secure the title as United narrowly lost out to Liverpool. Defeats to the men from Anfield and, ironically, Stoke derailed a potential title challenge as the Red Devils stumbled at Easter when they needed to keep a cool head.

It had been a huge improvement on the previous couple of seasons, with Busby sensing that his team were on the periphery of something great. Best was now settling in with his new team-mates and looked like he was a player with more than a hundred games under his belt rather than being a novice at the start of his career. The following year, the team struck gold. Law again provided the firepower, ably assisted by Best, Charlton,

Herd and Connelly. In fact, the goals scored by those players were just enough to edge Leeds United out on goal average, with the two teams both finishing at the top of the table on 61 points.

United's fate was effectively decided on Monday, 26 April 1965 when they defeated Arsenal 3-1 at Old Trafford. United's advantage on goal average over Leeds meant that Aston Villa would need to beat Busby's high-flying charges 19-0 in their last game of the season for the title to head over to Yorkshire. Frank McGhee of the *Daily Mirror* wrote: 'Manchester United are champions again. The five-word sentence manager Matt Busby has waited seven years to read became fact at 9.10pm last night with the final whistle of Old Trafford's last home game.'

Law and Best both notched, with the youngster gaining more plaudits, with McGhee describing Best's opening goal beautifully. 'Law, twisting on that injured knee to avoid a tackle, slipped the ball to Best. The kid trapped it calmly, swivelled towards the goal, paused almost cheekily to examine the situation, and then shot.' As it turned out, United lost 2-1 at Villa Park in their final game but the champagne corks had already been popped on what was a remarkable title-winning campaign.

The club's sixth top-flight championship meant that Busby would yet again lead his team into the European Cup, the first time since that fateful appearance in 1958.

United brushed past HJK Helsinki and Vorwärts Berlin in the opening two rounds, lining up a quarter-final tie with Portuguese powerhouse Benfica, who boasted the world-renowned forward Eusébio. A 3-2 win at Old Trafford set up a tense match in the return leg – but it would be a night when George Best introduced himself to the world.

Two goals from Best in the opening 11 minutes shocked the Portuguese side, who looked like a heavyweight boxer that had just been delivered a knockout blow; except, the referee didn't stop the fight, letting both boxers carry on until the final bell. When it rang, United had completed a demolition job, running out 5-1 victors on the night and securing a place in the semi-finals, where they would face Partizan Belgrade for a place in the showpiece.

Portuguese sports paper *A Bola* was scathing of Benfica and complimentary of United in its post-match report. 'For Benfica players and fans, it was a terrible nightmare. For those, however, who managed to put their affection for football above their club allegiance, and silenced the pain of defeat, it was a beautiful and unforgettable dream night. The Red Devils have cost us the cup but our dignity will remain as at least we know that we have lost to the best.'

Even the Benfica players were blown away by the events that had unfolded in front of their very eyes. 'A hurricane passed through the Luz that night and his name was George Best,' recalled António Simões, the Portugal and Benfica great. 'It was a terrible evening for us and an inspirational night for him. I can still see him arriving for his first goal, a header, to deflate our hopes. I still remember the headlines. We were not afraid – but that was *before* the game. Then we saw Best's genius, so unrestrained it was almost irresponsible.'

Superlatives were thrown at the 19-year-old United star across the continent and he was even dubbed 'El Beatle', a reflection of his new-found fame at a time when The Beatles were Britain's most famous export. Someone even managed to paint a picture depicting the pop quartet on the famous Abbey Road crossing photo but with Best added to the line-up. It was a crazy time but the forward knew this was exactly where he wanted to be.

Best remembered in his autobiography *Blessed*: 'This was the sort of stage I was meant to play on. It was perfect theatre. As I walked up the tunnel and heard the noise, the hair stood up on the back of my neck. But I didn't feel any fear. I wasn't in awe but I did know that I was ready. On nights like that, good players become great players and great players become gods. It was surreal stuff. I've seen other great teams play like that but to be a part of such an experience was unreal. Strangely, although I can replay almost the whole 90 minutes of that match in my head, I can't remember a single thing after the final whistle.'

Despite the stellar performance, there was hint of amusement surrounding the display, with Busby having claimed to the press prior to kick-off that United would be going there to 'keep it tight'. Best's team-mate, Bill Foulkes, would later recall: 'At half-time, I said to George "Didn't you hear the plan, then?" It was like George either hadn't heard or completely ignored Matt Busby's instruction to keep it tight. George just went out and did his own thing. It was like he was playing them on his own. I didn't go over the halfway line much, just stayed back to defend. Like everyone else that night, I just watched in wonder at the things George did.'

Football has an annoying habit of bringing you back down to earth and it was a case of 'after the Lord Mayor's Show' for Busby and his United team, as the final week in April would see the team's campaign completely derailed. Trailing Liverpool by a substantial margin in the title race, United were left to fight for the FA Cup and the European Cup. Everton and Partizan were semi-final opponents in the respective competitions, with Partizan the first to feature in United's double cup run-in. After a 2-0 defeat in Belgrade, United were unable to turn around the tie at Old Trafford, despite a Nobby Stiles goal, and another European dream was ended. Then, just three days later, the Toffees inflicted more misery on a United team who were now running on empty and were left trophyless.

With the team finishing only fourth in Division One at the end of that gruelling season, it meant there would be no European football for the 1966/67 campaign and, after early exits from both the FA and League Cup, United only had the First Division to concentrate their efforts on. Three defeats in the opening seven matches looked to have knocked the stuffing out of the team but a derby day victory in September ignited the season. Denis Law's strike against Manchester City in a 1-0 win was one of 25 goals the 'Lawman' scored in an assault on the league that ended with the trophy heading back to Old Trafford, with United pipping Nottingham Forest at the post. There was no late-season blow-up this time as Busby's men crossed the line in pole position.

It was the club's seventh top-flight title, with five of them coming under the stewardship of Matt Busby and his assistant, Jimmy Murphy, and it was clinched on Saturday, 6 May when United travelled to West Ham United and put them to the sword. The Red Devils were showing some swagger in their football, putting six goals past the hapless Hammers, who were unable to get anywhere near Busby's newly crowned champions. After the match, the United boss said: 'I asked everyone for a great effort at the start of the season and a great effort they have given me. My greatest ambition now is to bring home the European Cup.'

When the 1967/68 season kicked off, United set about defending their league title, as well as having the added bonus of the European Cup to look forward to. They resumed action in the summer of 1967, hosting the Charity Shield at Old Trafford against Tottenham Hotspur. An enthralling 3-3 draw with Spurs meant that the trophy was shared but it was certainly the curtain-raiser that the FA were hoping for to begin a new campaign. A week later, United were beaten 3-1 at Everton, which was not an ideal way to start a new league campaign. The men from Goodison Park seemingly held some kind of hoodoo over Busby and his team.

United soon kicked into gear and by the turn of the year, they were yet again sitting pretty at the top of the First Division. In the FA Cup, holders Tottenham were their FA Cup third round opponents and, after a replay, the Londoners inflicted a narrow defeat on Busby's men. In the league, Liverpool, Leeds United, and Manchester City were all coming up fast in United's rear-view mirror and there was little separating the four sides. A tricky March upset United's title charge when three defeats in four saw them slip back down to third position and open the door for the hunting pack.

Wins over Stoke City, Fulham and Sheffield United catapulted the Red Devils back to the summit with just three matches remaining, only for a shock 6-3 defeat at West Bromwich Albion to allow the Blues from across the city to leapfrog them at the top. City would go on to win their final two matches, pipping United at the post in a photo finish. It was a disappointing end to the season domestically, with the team stumbling at the worst possible time, but they had good reason to have taken their eyes off the ball, as their exploits on the European stage were running simultaneously.

Hibernians of Malta and Yugoslav champions FK Sarajevo were easily dispatched in the opening two rounds before a trickier tie against Górnik Zabrze from Poland. A 2-0 win in the first leg was followed by a 0-1 defeat in the second, with United made to sweat before eventually getting over the line. Coincidentally, that second-leg loss against the Polish team came in the few weeks when United couldn't seem to buy a win in any competition. It was a real temporary drop in form at a critical time but, like they eventually did in the league, they rallied again just in time for the semi-final first leg against Real Madrid.

More than 63,000 fans crammed into Old Trafford to see a single George Best goal separate the two sides before a nervy trip to the Santiago Bernabéu ten days later. It was a whirlwind of a tie, with the kings of Spain going full throttle against the cream of England. Madrid raced into a two-goal lead and looked to have caught United off guard but a freak own goal on the stroke of half-time brought the teams level on aggregate. The home side scored again almost instantly after the restart to give them a 3-1 advantage on the night and a 3-2 lead overall.

With less than 20 minutes left on the clock, United found a little something inside themselves that had been missing the previous few weeks and replied through David Sadler and Bill Foulkes, to turn the match on its head. United had won 4-3 on aggregate. It was a fantastic effort from Busby's team, who had gone into Madrid's own backyard and produced a monster performance when it looked like they were heading out of the competition. The team had recorded a memorable victory and one that gave them great confidence to push on and finally lift the trophy. All eyes were now on the final. United were the first English club to reach a European Cup Final and, by a happy coincidence, the 1968 final was to be held at Wembley Stadium.

United's opponents in the showpiece on 29 May 1968 were old foes Benfica, who were looking to avenge the humiliating defeat United had dealt them 18 months earlier. Busby's men, dressed in all royal blue, strode confidently across the Wembley pitch and, boy, were the supporters enjoying themselves on the terraces. It was a cagey first period, as you can imagine with so much riding on the outcome, but United were determined to put right the wrong of falling away late in the title race. Bobby Charlton scored shortly after half-time but the Portuguese side levelled through Graça with just ten minutes remaining. Neither team could then break the deadlock and extra time ensued.

Benfica looked dead on their feet while United seemed to just click into a higher gear and, within two minutes of the restart, United had scored twice through George Best and birthday boy Brian Kidd. A late Bobby Charlton goal, his second of the night, sealed a 4-1 win. It was a momentous occasion in the club's history, becoming the first English team to win the cup. Busby ran on to the pitch and hugged his players. He had been so close before to winning the European Cup and looked destined to achieve it ten years earlier had it not been for that horrific accident. Now he had realised that dream and the triumph was a tribute to those who had lost their lives in the Munich air disaster.

His players urged him to make his way to the royal box for the presentation of the trophy but the ever-so-modest manager politely refused, urging his heroes to go and take their bow in front of the red army who were still bellowing out their names. Busby eventually got his hands on the cup, held the trophy above his head said that it was 'the most wonderful thing to have happened in my life'. Busby reflected: 'I have had lots of disappointments but this has made up for everything. At the moment, I'm the proudest man in England.' Nobby Stiles looked exhausted as he walked around Wembley, doing his lap of honour. He had run his socks off. 'We were really shattered in extra time but so were Benfica and once we all sensed this, we really began to play.'

United had been the kings of England and now they were crowned the best team in Europe. It was a fitting way to end a final that was held on home soil. Once the dust had settled on the European Cup triumph, Matt Busby was knighted for his services to football, reflecting a successful 23-year period (and counting) in charge of Manchester United. Busby had seen his team win plenty of accolades but the knighthood was one for his own merit and one that was truly deserved, having faced, and overcome, adversity of the highest order. Manchester United were in safe hands as the curtain came down on the historic 1967/68 season … or so they thought.

The Hunger Years

PRIOR TO the start of the 1989/90 season, Manchester United had not tasted title-winning champagne for 22 years and were no closer to ending that drought with the team sitting in 15th place as we all sang 'Auld Lang Syne' to see in the start of a new decade on 1 January 1990. The club had gone for more than two decades without winning the First Division title and the pressure was becoming increasingly intense, year after year, as the team fought hard to get over the line. With the last championship season coming way back in 1966/67, it had been a tough watch for the Red Devils supporters, who had to endure the dominance of Liverpool throughout the 1970s and 80s. Not only were the Reds from down the East Lancs Road doing it on home soil, they were doing the business in Europe as well.

If you added into the mix European Cup wins for both Nottingham Forest and Aston Villa, following league titles for these clubs, then it was no wonder that everyone associated with Manchester United Football

Club was at breaking point. Forest even had the audacity to retain their European title, winning it back-to-back in 1979 and 1980. For United, there were so many false dawns along the way as the team tried to emulate what was considered the golden period in the club's history under the tenure of Sir Matt Busby. Something had to give soon.

Busby's side were riding the crest of a wave but like even the greatest surfers to ever grace a surfboard, you will eventually run out of sea as you land at the shoreline and that was exactly the case in the 1968/69 season. The previous campaign had been euphoric, no doubt. The European Cup triumph had completed a remarkable turnaround for the club but, just a few months later, the seams began to split on a team that had been playing at 100mph for nearly three years. Even the defence of their European crown couldn't seem to inspire the players as they crashed out at the semi-final stage to AC Milan.

Six defeats in the opening 14 league matches put paid to any sort of title charge and, with a further flurry of defeats coming in the December period to leave United floundering, Busby was left wondering if the magic had worn off his special side. With four defeats in five games over the Christmas period, there was a sense that something was bubbling under the surface and on 14 January 1969, that feeling soon turned to one of the problems boiling over. Sir Matt Busby announced that he was going to retire as manager at the end of the season after nearly a quarter of a century at the helm. It was a seismic declaration and one that shocked everyone associated with the club, as well as fans far and wide.

'It's time to make way for a younger man, a tracksuited manager,' Busby proclaimed to the press. 'United is no longer just a football club. It is an institution. I feel the demands are beyond one human being.' Ironically, United would go on to win their next game 4-1 at Old Trafford against Sunderland but would again fall into a poor run of form that would eventually see them finish in 11th position. The team were now not only losing a great manager in Busby but also a great person. He was fantastic with his players and those who were ready to fight for him.

Hugh McIlvanney of *The Observer* wrote a glowing reference of Sir Matt, who had retired from his position in the dugout and elevated himself into the role of general manager. 'The greatest fallacy about Busby is that his public behaviour has swollen around a soft centre of gentleness.' United player Pat Crerand, who had the sort of affinity with Busby that any other Catholic wing-half from the west of Scotland might be expected to have had, said: 'He's the hardest man in the world. When he wants to, he makes you feel that the whole club revolves around you. But when he bombs you out, you are the lowest of the low. In my six years at Old Trafford, I've never heard any player answer back. I don't care who you were, you'd go right out the door.'

Liam Whelan, a Manchester United forward who died at Munich, would have endorsed that belief. He once went into Busby's office and declared that he should be dropped from the first XI. Busby looked at him with that calculating seriousness that had withered more distinguished players and said: 'No one tells me who to put into my team and who to drop. I manage this side. If I keep you in, it is because you are playing the way I want you to. Keep playing that way and don't ever do this again.'

Nobby Stiles, United's World Cup-winning midfielder, was also quick to chip in with praise for his manager. 'The boss said it would take ten years to rebuild the team and in 1968, exactly ten years later, we won the European Cup.' Busby had just known he could turn the team's fortunes back around after those dark days that had engulfed the club had passed – and he did it. Now, there was going to be huge change at Old Trafford but, like anything in life, nothing lasts forever. Amid an avalanche of media interest over who would be taking up the post after Busby, it seemed that the position would be kept in-house and given to one of Sir Matt's loyal subjects. He wanted someone he could trust to lead the team back to the summit of English football and that man was right under his nose.

Wilf McGuinness had to call time on his playing career at just 22 years of age following a broken leg sustained during the 1959/60 season. McGuinness had broken into the first team at United just a few years earlier and, by a small twist of fate, missed the trip to Munich in 1958 through injury. Following his retirement, the wing-half stayed around the squad, helping Murphy with his coaching sessions before eventually joining Sir Matt's bench staff in 1964, assuming the role of reserve-team manager. Now, though, he was about to take on his biggest role of all and at the tender age of just 31.

McGuinness was chosen to replace Busby in a kind of 'better the devil you know' scenario. Such in-house managerial appointments would prove spot on for Liverpool in the 1970s and 1980s, with Bill Shankly handing over the reins to Bob Paisley, who then passed the mantle to Joe Fagan, another member of the famous 'Boot Room'. It was seamless, with the Anfield club hardly skipping a beat. But, at Old Trafford in 1969, McGuinness had the biggest of all shoes to fill when he took over from his old boss.

That was a daunting enough task for the incoming manager but there was another problem coming over the horizon in the form of the team itself, as it was heading into a transitional period. This was coupled with the star player now seemingly prioritising his rock 'n' roll lifestyle over the job that actually paid him a wage. George Best was beginning to be pictured on more front pages of tabloid newspapers than back pages. 'If you'd given me the choice of going out and beating four men and smashing a goal in from 30 yards against Liverpool or going to bed with Miss World, it would have been a difficult choice,' said Best. 'Luckily, I had both.' Despite his flamboyant displays off the pitch, Best still finished the 1969/70 season as the team's top scorer, with 24 goals in all competitions.

Three defeats in the opening four matches hardly inspired confidence as the team struggled to an eighth-place finish and exited domestic cup competitions at the semi-final stage. The start of the following campaign saw little to no improvement for the side as inconsistencies in form yet again derailed any chance of a title push. Five defeats in the opening 12 matches were deemed unacceptable by the board and, amid increasing pressure from the fans, McGuinness's job was hanging by a thread. A further string of defeats eventually saw the end of McGuinness's tenure, despite a rip-roaring 4-4 draw against Derby County on Boxing Day, with United coming back from four goals down.

Unfortunately, it wasn't enough to save the manager's job and by the turn of the year, McGuinness had returned to his original post of reserve-team manager. Sir Matt resumed the role on a temporary basis until the end of the season but, although results and performances improved, United had to settle for an eighth-place finish. 'Not everyone, sadly, would play for Wilf,' midfielder David Sadler told Eamon Dunphy in *A Strange Kind of Glory*. 'The side as a whole did not give 100 per cent effort for him. It was as simple as that. As soon as Sir Matt returned to the scene, it changed at once.'

The summer of 1971 saw a new face through the doors at Old Trafford in the shape of Frank O'Farrell, who signed a five-year contract to replace Busby, who was to resume his position overseeing operations. O'Farrell began his management career in the south-west, managing Weymouth before moving on to Torquay United. He enjoyed success with both clubs, leading Weymouth to the Southern Division championship and then guiding Torquay out of the Fourth Division as champions.

This alerted many to his talents and prompted Leicester City to opt for his services. He led the Foxes to the 1969 FA Cup Final, where they narrowly missed out to Manchester City, before guiding his team back to the First Division. From the success he had already gained in a short career in the dugout, it was clear that O'Farrell had something in his locker but the sticking point for many was that he had only achieved it at a lower level. This was Manchester United and just three years ago they were being hailed as the best team in Europe.

His tenure got off to an almost perfect start, a 1-0 defeat to Everton at Goodison Park the only defeat in his first 14 games. Best, Charlton and Law were thriving again and it showed on the pitch with some scintillating displays, with at least one of the trio finding the net in each match bar the loss on Merseyside. O'Farrell was named manager of the month for September and his side topped the table for the first time in three seasons. At one point, the team held a ten-point advantage over the chasing pack … but there was trouble brewing.

Despite the team starting like a train, O'Farrell's management style was beginning to wear thin with the players, most notably with George Best. It was reported that among the players' gripes was that they had to schedule a meeting with the boss if they wanted to have a chat with him. Best and O'Farrell had clearly bumped heads and when the mercurial forward failed to show up to a training session in early January, O'Farrell was forced to play without one of the 'Holy Trinity' and the wheels seemed to come off instantaneously. Best was United's ruthless game-winner and proved the difference against Ipswich, Derby and Newcastle. He hit hat-tricks against West Ham and Southampton and, by Christmas, United were sitting at the summit.

However, seven league defeats on the spin from New Year's Day saw United plummet down the table and sowed the first seeds of doubt over O'Farrell's leadership. His team would only win five matches from January onwards, finishing in eighth position for the third season running and, with tensions now running high between the manager and arguably the team's greatest player in Best, it was going to take something special to pull a rabbit out of the hat in the 1971/72 campaign. O'Farrell had spent big in his short time in charge, spending around £500,00 as he brought in Martin Buchan, Ian Storey-Moore, Wyn Davies and Ted MacDougall.

In May 1972, O'Farrell had to deal with yet another issue concerning Best. He announced in the press that he had decided to retire from football. The story was accompanied by a picture of Best at a villa in Marbella, sitting by the pool and sipping on a beer. It was a shock to everyone but, within a fortnight, Best rescinded his retirement and returned to meet the manager for clear the air talks. After the meeting, a friend asked how the conversation went.

'He talked about wolves,' Best replied.

'Wolves?' said the friend.

'Yes,' Best said.

'Something about the boy who cried wolf.'

Best was handed a two-week suspension from the club but the drama didn't stop there. Further altercations with Best meant that the Northern Ireland international would yet again undermine O'Farrell's preparations for matches, with the player continuing his no-show approach to training. The team's start to the season was a polar opposite to 12 months earlier, with the Red Devils winning only once in their opening 12 matches. Further defeats followed, heightening the pressure on the manager. When, in early December, O'Farrell decided Best had missed one too many training sessions, the player was transfer-listed.

By this time, morale amongst the players had hit rock bottom. Even the likes of Charlton and Law were struggling to give the team any momentum in games, with the side lacking any real threat at all, and when United crashed to a 5-0 defeat at Crystal Palace on 16 December 1972, O'Farrell was given his marching orders. On the same day that Best had left, the manager had followed him swiftly out of the door, leaving United rocking. In a strange turn of events, the future manager of Manchester United was already in the building, although he didn't know it at the time.

Tommy Docherty was managing the Scottish national team and had gone to United's match at Selhurst Park to take a look at a Crystal Palace full-back for his upcoming squad selection, only to be told on the gate that there was no room in the inn. O'Farrell made some calls and managed to lay his hands on a couple of complimentary tickets for Docherty, who would view the match from the directors' box. It was here that Docherty would be approached about the prospect of managing United, with O'Farrell unaware he was managing his last game for the club.

'I felt awful, so sorry for him,' Docherty told *RTÉ*, 'Because I knew that the job was mine if I wanted it. I thought "Should I tell him?"'

O'Farrell thought that it was a 'lovely day for an execution' when he went in to meet the United chairman on 19 December. He was told that his contract was being terminated because of the club's position near the bottom of the league. United were hovering precariously above the relegation zone but Docherty still saw enough in the side to accept the role, starting his position just a few days later.

Following his sacking, O'Farrell blamed internal matters at the club, claiming that the people he dealt with inside United 'weren't very nice people' and that Sir Matt Busby was 'one of the worst of them'. Busby always denied direct interference but many felt his presence undermined his immediate successors. In his 1973 memoir, *Soccer at the Top*, Busby directly addressed those who felt he should have stepped aside completely. 'How could I leave the place? How could I walk out of a club I built on the ashes of war and rebuilt after the mass tragedy of Munich, a club I love dearly, a club I have nearly killed myself for?'

Docherty arrived having previously won the League Cup as manager of Chelsea, as well as managing abroad with FC Porto, but this was going to be the biggest task that the Scot would face.

The team were struggling for goals and the 'Holy Trinity' of Best, Law and Charlton were, respectively, AWOL, injured and close to retirement. Charlton finished the campaign as the team's highest goalscorer with a grand total of just six. Law had been struggling with injuries and was eventually allowed to join Manchester City. Best was exiled from the club and, although he was given a reprieve under the new boss, it wasn't the same.

A flurry of wins towards the tail end of the season papered over a few cracks, with the team managing to scrape an 18th-place finish but the worst was yet to come, just 12 months later. The team were entering an enormous transition period and, only five seasons after the ecstasy of the European Cup triumph, United ran out of steam and crashed through the trapdoor and into the Second Division for the first time since 1938. Thirty-odd years of hard work had been undone but the club had pulled together in adversity and fought its way back before and that's exactly what Docherty and Co. were about to do again. United began that fateful 1973/74 season with two wins in their opening three games but then managed only four wins in the next 20 league matches between September and March. A late-season run of victories raised the possibility of survival, but United could only delay the inevitable for so long and relegation was confirmed.

United's final home match was against their city rivals, with the Red Devils desperate for a win to stave off the threat of relegation. A 0-1 defeat, sealed by a Denis Law backheel, ended any chance of survival. Law looked disinterested in celebrating as he walked back to the halfway line. Hordes of United supporters stormed the pitch in an effort to the get game abandoned but the attempt at such was all in vain. Legend has it that Law relegated United that day, much to the delight of rival supporters. In fact, it was Birmingham City's win over Norwich City and West Ham United's point against Liverpool that sealed United's fate. With a win still worth only two points, United could not have caught Birmingham and West Ham even if they had won their last two fixtures.

The season had been a rollercoaster for both the club and the fans. George Best had been sent packing midway through the campaign, with the manager finally losing patience with the United star and Best finally signing off from Old Trafford after ten years of service. Goalkeeper Alex Stepney had at one stage in the season led the goalscoring charts due to becoming the club's penalty taker, bizarrely having scored one in a pre-season friendly. 'It was about six or seven games into the season,' Stepney told *Manutd.com*. 'I think we were at home on the Wednesday night and Gerry Daley used to take penalties but he failed a fitness test. When the bell went to go out, we said who was taking any penalties and Martin, the captain, said "Alex".

'And then we played Birmingham,' he added. 'It was down to me to run from the Stretford End to the Scoreboard End, as it was in those days, and beat Mike Kelly, who was the Birmingham goalkeeper. In all due respect, I was getting my own back because, when I was an amateur, I played for Tooting & Mitcham and our local derby was against Wimbledon and Mike was their goalkeeper at the time. And then I went to Millwall and he was with Queens Park Rangers and I think they beat us, too, so, at last, I got my own back!'

Stepney held the position of top scorer for ten matches before Lou Macari and Sammy McIlroy finally managed to catch up, highlighting just how much the team were faltering in front of goal during that period. Despite the club dropping down a division, Docherty was given a vote of confidence, with the board believing he would gain promotion at the first time of asking. The team needed a complete overhaul but still had plenty of quality for the second tier, securing the championship with an impressive run towards the end of the campaign, although they were pushed all the way by an also impressive Aston Villa.

Docherty had shelled out for Stuart Pearson in the summer of 1974 and the ex-Hull City forward proved to be the catalyst as the Red Devils returned to the top table of English football after a one-year hiatus. 'Pancho', with his famous raised right fist celebration after scoring, contributed more than 30 goals between 1974 and 1976, culminating in United not only regaining their First Division status but also threatening to make it two championships in a row before three defeats in their final five matches derailed a surprise title charge for Docherty's swashbuckling, new-look side, narrowly missing out to Liverpool as the team finished in a surprisingly impressive third place. United also reached the 1976 FA Cup Final against Second Division Southampton but when the Saints went marching in, they upset the odds with a hugely controversial (miles offside) goal in a 1-0 win.

The manager was defiant, despite a slight blip in an otherwise near flawless season. 'We'll be back next year,' he announced from the balcony of the town hall in Manchester's Albert Square, 'and this time we'll win it.' He wasn't wrong. A year later, United were once again heading to the twin towers, this time for a showdown with a dominant Liverpool who were bidding for an unprecedented Treble of league title, FA Cup and European Cup. It was a tie that certainly sharpened the minds of the United players, who were desperate not to walk up those Wembley steps again to collect yet another runners-up medal.

'I think we could have won the league the year before,' remembers Martin Buchan, the United captain. 'But we got distracted by the cup. Then, on that day, certain players felt all they had to do was turn up to win it. Against Liverpool, you would never adopt that kind of attitude.' In an article in *The Independent*, United midfielder Lou Macari said: 'I think it helped us enormously that we were the underdogs. I cannot remember Manchester United being the underdogs ever but, in that game, when you looked at the two teamsheets, you had to accept the bookies' assessment.'

If you had put your rent on the favourites that day, you would have had to have hidden behind the sofa when the landlord came to collect his money, as a 2-1 win by United brought Docherty's proclamation to life. Goals from Pearson and Jimmy Greenhoff, who had a knack of scoring important goals that campaign, were enough to topple the Reds from Merseyside and end a nine-year wait for a major trophy … the last being that beautiful European Cup triumph. It was the club's fourth FA Cup win, even if it did come with a touch of fortune for the winning goal. Macari thought he had snatched the glory, only to be told later on that he was going to be the bridesmaid at this particular wedding.

'At the time, there was an award of a golden boot trophy for the player who scored the winner,' he recalls. 'I thought "That'll do nicely, cup winner's medal and the golden boot". I was on my way to the dressing room when I saw Jimmy Greenhoff carrying it and I thought to myself "Why have they given it to him? Maybe he's just holding on to it for me for safe keeping". So, I went up to him and asked him what he was doing with it. He thought I was taking the mickey, but I honestly didn't know until that point what had happened.'

His comment was in reference to United's second goal of the game, which proved to be the winner, with Macari firing in a shot and wheeling away in delight as it hit the back of the Wembley net. The reality was that his strike had actually taken a wicked deflection off the chest of Greenhoff, bamboozling Ray Clemence in the Liverpool goal. Regardless of that slice of good fortune for United, it was a fantastic result. Just 12 months after his last visit to Manchester Town Hall, Docherty was back again. 'This,' he said, raising the trophy high into the Manchester sky to the delight of the doting thousands, 'is the start of something big.'

Speaking to the *Sunday Mirror*, Docherty said 'I've waited 26 years for this – and would you believe it, I just don't feel a thing, it hasn't sunk in yet. This was my eighth visit to Wembley, five as a player and third as a manager and it's the first time I have been a winner.' Docherty's celebrations and plans of turning United into world beaters were about to be cut short soon after the FA Cup Final victory, with allegations that the boss was having an extra-marital affair with the wife of the club physio. The accusations did, in fact, turn out to be true and just weeks later, in July 1977, Docherty was axed as Manchester United manager.

His successor, ironically, was the man who had replaced him when he left his role at Chelsea. Dave Sexton took over from Docherty and was charged with taking the team forward. Sexton had won the FA Cup with Chelsea, as well as the European Cup Winners' Cup, but had a reputation for falling out with his players, selling Chelsea hero Peter Osgood before overseeing the club's relegation, resulting in him picking up his P45. He was a fag paper away from winning the First Division title with his next club, Queens Park Rangers, in 1975/76 but Liverpool pipped them at the post, culminating in QPR finishing second, their highest ever finish, even to this day. His recruitment was a shrewd move from the United board, or so they thought, but the fans didn't take to the playing style brought in, with many calling it slow and pedestrian with very little risk. The players looked robotic in their performances, with the manager dictating every move.

One of the casualties under the new manager was Gordon Hill. 'Merlin', the charismatic forward who had charmed the United faithful with his exquisite wing play, was shown the door. When he was sold to Derby County in 1978, supporters already unconvinced by the man in the dugout really began to sway against Sexton. United finished tenth in Sexton's first season, with the departing Hill the top scorer in all competitions with 19 goals … even more reason for the confusion among fans.

Sexton set about shaping his squad by relying heavily on the club's cheque book.

Scottish international forward Joe Jordan was signed from Leeds United and managed double figures in his maiden season, chipping in with ten goals in all competitions as United yet again failed to find any consistency in the league, culminating in another mid-table position, this time ninth place. Luckily for Sexton, the team seemed to click into gear in the FA Cup, defeating his old club, Chelsea, and Tottenham

Hotspur before seeing off arch rivals Liverpool to reach the Wembley showpiece against Arsenal.

The 1979 FA Cup Final was to become known as the 'five-minute final' after a mad end to the match that left spectators aghast. Arsenal had led their opponents 2-0 until United rallied late on with two goals in the last five minutes from Gordon McQueen and Sammy McIlroy to send the game towards extra time … or so they thought. With United having clawed their way back into the game, it looked like Sexton's men were going to be rewarded for their hard work, only for an 89th-minute winner from Alan Sunderland to break United hearts and secure the Gunners the trophy. It was a real kick in the teeth for Sexton who, from the brink of disaster, had somehow managed to gain a lifeline, only for it to be cruelly snatched away in the dying embers of the match. The result kind of summed up Sexton's tenure, to be honest.

That summer, the manager broke the club's transfer record when he signed Ray Wilkins from Chelsea for a fee believed to be around the £800,000 mark. The midfielder was a slick operator and almost instantly changed United's approach to matches with his efficient distribution of the football in the middle of the park. Wilkins was way ahead of his time in the way that he played and would be considered a Rolls-Royce player in today's game, in which teams like to dominate the ball. Sexton's team pushed Liverpool all the way but were unable to stop the Reds from Merseyside claiming their fifth title in eight seasons. Despite only trailing Liverpool by two points at the end of the campaign, the damage had already been done in the early part of the season after a shaky start.

Sexton, feeling he was closing in on securing a league title, again splashed the cash, this time a British record fee of around £1.25m on Nottingham Forest's red-hot marksman, Garry Birtles. His 32 goals in 83 appearances for the Tricky Trees alerted the attention of the boss but the player who came through the door at Old Trafford was certainly not the same one who was scoring for fun at the City Ground. Birtles only found the net once (in an FA Cup tie) in 28 appearances as the Red Devils struggled to put games to bed, drawing 18 times that season. It all ended with another disappointing finish – eighth this time. The team's foray into the UEFA Cup ended with a whimper as the club crashed out on away goals in round one to the very unfancied Widzew Łódź.

Despite spending over £2m, Sexton had seemingly taken the team backwards, having not capitalised on the runner-up campaign in 1979/80 and, in the summer of 1981, he was relieved of his duties. Martin Edwards had taken over the role of chairman after his father, Louis, passed away from a heart attack a year earlier, having been in charge since 1965. Now it was time for Edwards junior to make his first big decision. 'I felt that Dave had had four years in charge and that United were not progressing,' admitted Edwards. 'We were no nearer to winning the league. I also felt that the supporters were a little bit disgruntled with the style of football we were playing. We had some very poor attendances that season [attendances dropped from 54,394 on the opening day of the season to 40,165 on the final day]. So, I decided to dismiss Dave, my first major decision. I know that some players were not happy but I felt it was right. The board saw me act decisively and I felt stronger in the position from then on.'

The club were now on the lookout for a new man. Southampton's Lawrie McMenemy, who had masterminded his club's shock FA Cup win over United in 1976, was high on the list of candidates and had even given Edwards his word before doing a U-turn and committing his future at The Dell. 'I'd spoken to him and he indicated that he would come to United,' Edwards said. 'McMenemy then rang me and told me that his wife didn't want to move to Manchester and that he would not be coming. That left me in the lurch. My second choice was Bobby Robson. I spoke to him and he said that, while he was very flattered, he had unfinished business at Ipswich. He explained that he had a young squad with players he had brought in and he didn't want to leave them.'

This left Edwards scratching his head at his next move. 'The next choice was Ron Saunders,' said Edwards. 'He'd been successful and led [Aston] Villa to the 1980/81 championship but he wasn't interested and turned us down flat.' United were a different proposition then, which explains Saunders's reluctance even to discuss the job. 'While it was a big club, success was lacking. Between 1968 and 1983, the club won just one trophy, the FA Cup in 1977. It was a bleak period. United didn't have enough money in the kitty, either. Managers asked me how much money there would be. I was honest. They weighed up what I said and turned us down.'

Eventually, after a chance meeting with journalist John Maddock, a solution was found when he suggested taking a look at Ron Atkinson, who was the manager at West Bromwich Albion. Atkinson had been in charge of the Baggies since 1978 and in his short time at the helm, had already moulded his team to play some scintillating football. His first full season with the club heralded a third-place finish in the First Division which in turn meant that the Baggies would be playing European football the following campaign in the form of the UEFA Cup. Atkinson led his team to the quarter-finals of that competition. He also masterminded a 5-3 humbling of Dave Sexton's United at Old Trafford in December 1978 before WBA finished in fourth place during his final year in charge at the club.

Atkinson had the prospect of another season of European football at The Hawthorns but the lure of Manchester United was too great for 'Big Ron', who decided his future lay at Old Trafford. The playing style of his teams mirrored more the Tommy Docherty approach than that of Sexton and this excited the fans almost immediately. His management style, however, was a more laid-back approach, with the onus on his players to provide the magic, rather than orchestrating it for them. He seemed confident, flamboyant and ready for the challenge ahead.

Upon his arrival during the summer of 1981, Atkinson was quick to make changes to his squad, with the outgoings of Joe Jordan and Sammy McIlroy (who left several months later after 13 years at the club) who headed to AC Milan and Stoke City respectively. This was followed by the signing of Frank Stapleton from Arsenal, coupled with the arm round the shoulder of Garry Birtles, who must have thought his days were numbered following his barren first season in front of goal.

What Atkinson found in his squad was a mixture of players who had been through the Docherty era and some that had been brought in by Sexton. Moulding them all together quickly was going to be a challenge in itself. With the new signings settling in almost immediately, the players soon took to Atkinson's enthusiasm and his 'short, sharp' training sessions at The Cliff. 'Nothing was deliberate – you're just yourself,' said Atkinson. 'People said to me "You must have been very nervous?" No. If you don't want the job, you don't take it. It's somewhere you go and relish it. I never thought it was a crime to enjoy what you're doing and I think that rubbed off on the players. I used to enjoy going in every day.'

United got off to a decent start in 1981/82 and strengthened the engine room further with Atkinson signing both of his old central midfielders from WBA. Remi Moses joined for around £500,00 but what was soon going to be the jewel in United's crown was the acquisition of Bryan Robson for a British record fee of around £1.5m. 'The big aim was always to bring in Bryan Robson,' Atkinson told *M.E.N Sport*. 'It's common knowledge that I always said Robbo was the best player I ever worked with and I worked with some terrific players. I remember saying to the board of directors "This is not even a gamble. It's guaranteed".'

England international Robson was only 24 years old and had already suffered two broken legs and a dislocated ankle in his short career but his old boss knew quality when he saw it and, after much haggling between the two clubs, the deal was finally done, which included the signing of Robson being made on that now famous little white table that was placed on the Old Trafford pitch. In Robson's 2006 autobiography, *Robbo*, the midfielder said: 'When we arrived at Old Trafford, I wasn't disappointed. Martin Edwards offered me more than I had hoped for – £2,000 a week. The financial details were tied up and there were no hitches with the medical. It was a pity we missed the five o'clock deadline for me to be eligible to play that Saturday but I was relieved all the wrangling had finished. The following day, I was officially introduced as a United player at a press conference and on the Saturday formally signed on the dotted line, out on the Old Trafford pitch before United's home game against Wolverhampton Wanderers. A crowd of nearly 47,000 gave me a fantastic reception. Money wasn't my main motivation. I simply wanted to be a winner.'

Under Atkinson, even Birtles began to find the net, scoring 11 goals during the campaign but, as good a start as the team made, Liverpool (who were mid-table at Christmas) turned the screw in the second half of the season and romped to yet another championship. United and Atkinson finished in third spot, nestling just behind Bobby Robson's stylish Ipswich Town side, meaning that qualification to the UEFA Cup had been achieved. A youngster from Northern Ireland had also made his debut towards the tail end of the season, which showed that despite the marquee signings there were some decent players coming through the ranks.

When he stepped on to the pitch at the Goldstone Ground against Brighton & Hove Albion on 24 April 1982, Norman Whiteside became the youngest first-team player to make a United debut since Duncan Edwards back in 1953. Just a few weeks later, during the final match of the season, Whiteside, at the tender age of just 17, found the net in a 2-0 win over Stoke City to become the club's youngster-ever goalscorer.

Unfortunately for Birtles, this more or less signalled the end of his time at United, with the wildly inconsistent forward heading back to Nottingham Forest.

During the summer of 1982, Atkinson pulled off another shrewd signing in the shape of Ipswich Town midfielder Arnold Muhren on a free transfer. The Dutchman had been instrumental in Ipswich's remarkable UEFA Cup success, as well as helping the team to two First Division runners-up positions and was deemed an absolute steal. Muhren slotted in seamlessly as the team began the campaign in a decent vein of form, winning six of their opening ten matches, with a defeat at Atkinson's old club, West Brom, the only blot on the early-season copybook.

The manager's decision to give 17-year-old Whiteside a starring role was also paying dividends as the youngster bagged four goals in his opening five games. The league campaign did, however, tail off as they headed into the business end of the season, with four defeats in the last eight games meaning a third-place finish would have to do for the second consecutive year. Liverpool had again run away with the title while United were pipped to a silver medal by Graham Taylor's high-flying Watford team, who had just been promoted from the Second Division.

It was far from doom and gloom around the place, as the cup competitions were where the team seemed to really shine and, with this meaning a vast number of games, it was maybe a case of a little bit of exhaustion creeping in to curtail United's title challenge. The club had reached the League Cup Final for the first time in their history, courtesy of a 6-3 semi-final aggregate victory over Arsenal, and it would be old foes Liverpool who would await them in the showpiece. This was followed in the FA Cup by yet another semi-final win over the Gunners, who must have been sick of the sight of United. Unfancied Brighton & Hove Albion were to be their opponents in the final.

In the League Cup Final, Norman Whiteside gave United a great start. The lad from Northern Ireland struck inside 12 minutes, bamboozling Alan Hansen with a beautiful turn on the edge of Liverpool's penalty area before slotting into the bottom-right corner. Alan Kennedy fired a low, raking shot past Gary Bailey with just 15 minutes to go before an extra time winner from Ronnie Whelan broke United hearts. It was another cruel way to lose a final following the pain of defeat in 1979, with the absence of Bryan Robson a noticeable factor.

Fast Forward two months and the Red Devils were back under the twin towers of Wembley, this time to take on the Seagulls. Brighton had just been relegated from the top flight, so, unlike the League Cup Final, this time it was United who were the red-hot favourites to lift the trophy. But, boy, were they made to sweat. Robson was available this time but Brighton hadn't read the script when Gordon Smith found the net in the opening exchanges. Frank Stapleton pulled the teams level before a beautiful curling shot from Ray Wilkins had United on the brink with 18 minutes remaining.

Brighton rallied in the dying embers of the match and, in the 87th minute, won a corner following a short spell of pressure. The cross rolled across the 18-yard box before a low scuffed drive fell at the feet of Gary Stevens to rifle home the equaliser and send the fans in blue and white into ecstasy; 2-2. The game continued into extra time and with less than a minute to go in the match, Brighton must have thought they had snatched it. A long through ball from Jimmy Case was met by the lung-bursting run of Robinson. The Seagulls No.9 turned the trailing United defender inside out, opening up the goal for a shot but unselfishly he rolled it across to his strike partner Smith – only for Brighton's opening scorer to take one touch too many and fire it straight at the onrushing Bailey. Fantastic save, or horror miss? I'll let you decide that.

'I still put my money on United,' was the headline on the piece written by Frank McGhee for the *Daily Mirror* on the Monday after the final. 'No one, inside or outside of football, could have forecast correctly – and no one did – the result, the events, the heroes, the villains, the drama. No one for a start dared to hope that the 1983 FA Cup Final could possibly be as exciting and compelling, as tough, and as close, as it was. And only the stubbornly foolhardy could now feel as absolutely certain as I do that Manchester United, still, and always basically the better side, will win Thursday's replay.'

In the replay, United were not about to make the same mistake twice by underestimating their opponents and were three goals to the good before half-time. Whiteside scored a goal sandwiched in between two strikes from Robson, the Northern Irishman becoming the youngest player to have scored in both the League Cup and FA Cup finals. It was a real captain's performance from Robson and a greater show of the man was yet to come. United were awarded a penalty in the 62nd minute but instead of taking it himself and potentially scoring a hat-trick, Robson threw the ball to Muhren, who slotted home his spot kick to put the game to bed.

'People ask if I regret not taking it but I don't,' Robson told *Mail Sport*. 'I'd have had no qualms about it. Ray Wilkins threw the ball to me but we'd decided Arnold would take penalties. He never missed in training. It was only afterwards I realised he'd never taken one in a game for us or for Ipswich.' The 4-0 win secured United's first trophy in six seasons since Docherty's team won the FA Cup in 1977 but it was Gary Stevens of Brighton who took the plaudits in the match, winning the BBC man of the match award, much to the annoyance of the United manager. 'Ron Atkinson presented it in the TV interview room and said it was an "absolute joke" because Bryan Robson should have won it,' said Stevens. 'Typical Big Ron, throwing a bucket of water on my fire.'

The 1983/84 campaign got off to a decent start, with a 2-0 win over Liverpool in the Charity Shield followed up with eight wins in the opening 11 league matches to put United at the front of the pack. Atkinson's side managed to go from early December until the final day in March without tasting defeat before yet again succumbing to his former club, West Brom, at The Hawthorns to end a decent run in the First Division. Despite this, draws were becoming the Achilles' heel for the team and they would eventually fall away to finish in fourth place as Liverpool claimed another title. The season had shown glimpses of real promise, including wins over Liverpool and Arsenal, the latter being given a four-goal drubbing.

The defence of the FA Cup, on the other hand, was something of a damp squib. Drawn against Third Division Bournemouth, United headed to Dean Court looking to swat away the Cherries and march into round four. However, when they arrived on the south coast, it was a giant-killing that awaited them in the shape of an embarrassing 2-0 defeat. It was rumoured that Atkinson hadn't taken the game seriously, with rival manager Harry Redknapp suggesting his opposite number was in complacent mood telling his players: 'Atkinson did an interview and it came across like this game was an exercise.'

It was a notion that United full-back Arthur Albiston refuted when quizzed on the comments. 'We really wanted to win,' Albiston insisted. 'We were nowhere near winning the league at that time, so the cup was really important to us. Our attitude wasn't bad but we never got going, even though we were at full strength.' Whether Atkinson had taken his lower league counterparts lightly, no one knows, but he certainly didn't make the same mistake as the team waded through the early rounds of the European Cup Winners' Cup. Having dispatched Dukla Prague and Spartak Varna in the opening two rounds, it was into the quarter-finals and a showdown with Barcelona.

The side from Catalonia boasted a raft of top players, including the special talents of Bernd Schuster and Diego Maradona. United were pulled apart in the Camp Nou and were lucky to return to Manchester only two goals behind but what happened on the night of 21 March 1984 was something magical and arguably the greatest victory ever earned at the 'Theatre of Dreams'. More than 58,000 fans crammed into the stands to watch Atkinson's side battle back and overhaul the two-goal deficit and, against all odds, sail victorious into the semi-finals with a 3-0 victory.

Midfielder Ray Wilkins remembered the match fondly in his later years. Speaking to *United Review*, Wilkins said: 'I was lucky to have a long career in football and to play in some massive matches but I have never experienced a night like the one when we beat Barcelona 3-0 at Old Trafford. We had lost 2-0 at the Nou Camp, where Barça had hammered us, but we were looking forward to the return in the hope of turning things round. However, there was some trepidation as they were so gifted, with players such as Diego Maradona and Bernd Schuster.'

Wilkins had been instrumental in his link-up play with fellow England international Bryan Robson and it was clear for all to see, with his decisive passing and neat build-up play. 'Norman Whiteside nodded on my corner for Bryan Robson to score with a diving header at the far post for our opener,' said Wilkins. 'We then scored twice in three minutes early in the second half. I ought to have scored the aggregate equaliser but scuffed my shot, which came back off their keeper (Javier Urruticoechea) and Robbo slotted home to make it 2-2 overall. When Frank Stapleton banged home our third, the noise was incredible. I will never forget that, as it was really something to behold. Maradona then had a last-minute free kick that just flew the wrong side of the post. Thankfully, we held on for what still ranks as one of the club's finest victories over two legs.'

Italian giants Juventus were United's opponents in the final four and, playing without the injured Robson and the suspended Wilkins, the Red Devils crashed out 3-2 on aggregate, again highlighting inconsistencies in the team's performances, given the heroics in the previous round. It was something that was beginning to plague Atkinson's side, who were able to navigate one-off cup ties but seemed unable to commit to a sustained run of form during a league season and it was a trend that continued in the 1984/85 season.

Wilkins had departed the club, heading to the bright lights of Milan to sign for AC, and United had to fight tooth and nail to hold on to their captain, who looked destined to follow Wilkins to Italy. Juventus had been impressed by Robson's heroics against Barcelona and were granted permission to speak to United's No.7 after the second leg of the semi-final in Turin. 'We turned down an offer for Bryan Robson when he was at his absolute peak,' said chairman Martin Edwards. 'It was Juventus who were in for him and they offered £3m, which was a big sum at the time, but we didn't want Robson to go.' Luckily for everyone associated with the club, Robson stayed and continued his love affair with the Red Devils.

Following the departure of Wilkins, Atkinson decided to bolster his wing options rather than the central midfield area, signing Jesper Olsen and Gordon Strachan from Ajax and Aberdeen, respectively. Alan Brazil was brought in from Ipswich, another who had found the net with ease at his previous club but, like Birtles before him, never hit the ground running at Old Trafford. This was because of the emergence of youngster Mark Hughes from the youth team. The young Welshman was brought into the first-team attack to partner Frank Stapleton, with Norman Whiteside dropping back into midfield. Whiteside had that flair and ability that meant he could adopt to a number of positions with ease, a real gem for Atkinson.

United began the campaign with five draws in their opening seven matches before a flurry of defeats between October and New Year's Day completely derailed another title charge. Although Atkinson's men stayed in the hunt, they never really looked like reaching the summit. Like Docherty before him, Atkinson played an attacking brand of football, with the team urged to get on the front foot, but sometimes this cavalier attitude can come back to haunt you. Hughes finished his maiden season in double figures as yet again United finished fourth, with draws ultimately their undoing. The UEFA Cup run seemed to be gaining momentum following decent wins over PSV Eindhoven and Dundee United before a shock exit to the less-than-fancied Videoton of Hungary on penalties sent United crashing out in the quarter-finals.

Once again, it was an FA Cup run that saved the season as United breezed through the early stages until a semi-final meeting with Liverpool at Goodison Park that proved to be a cup tie for the ages. Atkinson seemed to have a hoodoo over Liverpool and, 1983 League Cup Final apart, was dominant over the Reds in both league and cup meetings. Liverpool had just reached another European Cup Final but would have wanted one of the other semi-final ties rather than United at this point. It was also pointed out that

Liverpool had not won the FA Cup in more than ten years, which was strange considering their domination in nearly every other competition. This was going to be some match.

Robson put United ahead in the 69th minute, arriving at the perfect time to fire home following a flick-on from a corner, and that looked to be enough to send Atkinson and his charges through to the final, only for Ronnie Whelan to equalise with just minutes remaining to send the match into extra time. It was a carbon copy of his League Cup winner but United needed to dust themselves down quickly, and not allow Liverpool to build up a head of steam. Stapleton scored via a deflection during the first period to give United the lead once more but again Liverpool found a way to claw themselves back into the match thanks to a Paul Walsh goal in the dying seconds.

A replay just four days later was required to separate the two sides. This time, the venue was Maine Road and if you thought that the atmosphere the first time around was electric, then this was on another planet. Liverpool boss Joe Fagan had realised that his team were lucky to still be in the competition. 'We didn't really deserve what we got,' he said. 'When they went 2-1 ahead in the first half of extra time, I felt we could all go home, so I am very thankful we have got another crack at it.' And when Paul McGrath put through his own net to give Liverpool the lead heading into half-time in the replay,

Fagan must have been counting his blessings over the turnaround in their fortunes.

Now, my dad used to say to me that, back then, if Bryan Robson didn't play, then more often than not United wouldn't win. This was why he was given the nickname 'Captain Marvel', with his momentous performance against Barcelona a year earlier the case in point. With just 45 minutes left on the clock, the team needed a big performance and who else but the man himself stepped up and gave us one. Winning the ball back from Kenny Dalglish, Robson played a quick one-two with Stapleton on the halfway line before hot-footing it through the Liverpool defence and, with Hansen and Co. bearing down on him, unleashing a 25-yarder straight into the top right-hand corner.

It was a truly fantastic strike and one that would have sent modern day social media into meltdown. United were level in the tie and just moments later, they took the lead. Gordon Strachan's defence-splitting pass set Hughes away, who fired low to beat Bruce Grobbelaar. There looked to be a hint of offside but no one from Manchester could care less that the linesman kept his flag down. The game ebbed and flowed as Liverpool looked to find a way back into the match but eventually the referee brought an end to the proceedings and, with a punch of the air from Atkinson, United headed to yet another cup final under his tenure. The United fans flooded on to the pitch at the home of their city rivals, desperate to congratulate their heroes in white, and for the second time in 12 months, Robson was hoisted upon the shoulders of the supporters and carried across the pitch. It made a change, someone carrying Robson for once.

Rob Smyth, reporting for *The Guardian*, wrote: 'This was football as nature intended, a relentlessly attacking slugfest played by proper men in front of proper men, effortlessly shivers the spine.' Steve Curry of the *Daily Express* said it was a 'raw embodiment of the best that British football has to offer'. Liverpool's city rivals, Everton, had reached the final, looking to claim a Treble of First Division, European Cup Winners' Cup and FA Cup. The first two of the three had been achieved when they met United in May 1985 but the Toffees were second favourites to add to their already impressive trophy haul.

On display in the showpiece were some exceptional talents. Everton midfielder Peter Reid, the PFA Players' Player of the Year, Mark Hughes, the PFA Young Player of the Year and the Football Writers' Association Player of the Year, Everton keeper Neville Southall. 'United will, I believe, take the trophy because they have more of the many individual talents on display – Bryan Robson, Mark Hughes, Jesper Olsen, Gordon Strachan to name the main four,' wrote Frank McGhee for the *Daily Mirror*. Derek Potter of the *Daily Express* took United to win by a couple of goals, whereas his colleague, Steve

Curry, although a lifelong United supporter, predicted that Everton would complete the Treble. Liverpool legend Phil Neal felt Everton's wide men would be the main difference on the day but anyone backing United that day must have feared the worst as the game developed.

A pretty forgettable first half was about to be replaced by an historic second. Andy Gray came close for the Toffees before Whiteside found Southall in imperious form as he raced on to a through ball, coming out second best to arguably the best keeper in the world at the time. Then in the 77th minute, a moment of history as Reid's heavy touch seemed to take the ball away from himself and, with Kevin Moran steaming in, he just about managed to nick the ball away from the United central defender, who in turn sent Reid spinning through the air and sprawling on to the Wembley turf. In today's era, with Moran being deemed the last man – albeit he was on the edge of the centre circle – it would have been a certain red card for the Republic of Ireland international. But back then, such an offence was generally deemed a yellow card at worst.

Referee Peter Willis called Moran towards him and what follows are the iconic lines from commentator Brian Moore and co-commentator Ian St John as Willis flashed a red card at the shellshocked United man. 'Oh! He's sent him off. He's sent Moran off,' gasped a shocked Moore, with St John equally surprised. 'I really do find that incredible, Brian. I think the referee is 100 per cent out of order.' It was the first time a player had been dismissed in an FA Cup Final and Moran left the pitch holding back the tears. Speaking to the press after the match, Willis doubled down on his decision, despite the clamour for justice. 'I have no second thoughts about sending off Kevin Moran. I believe I was right at the time and I still believe I was right. But that doesn't stop me feeling terrible about it.'

So, with United down to ten men, Atkinson rolled the dice. It was going to be all or nothing, against all the odds. As if the task in hand wasn't difficult enough, now it was a mountain to climb. The manager opted against bringing on a defender to plug the gap and, instead, moved Stapleton into the backline. United held strong and there was to be an additional 30 minutes played, with both sides looking dead on their feet. Everton huffed and puffed but a gruelling season looked to have caught up with them and they were unable to make their numerical advantage count. Atkinson must have been praying for a replay when he saw his centre-half dismissed but, as the game ticked towards its conclusion, his thought process was about to change significantly.

A Hughes pass with the outside of his boot sent Whiteside down the right wing. Pat van den Hauwe was there for company but the Blues defender just kept backing off and, before he could engage, Whiteside cut inside on to his trusty left foot and curled a beautiful shot past Southall and into the far bottom corner. Steve Curry would later observe: 'You need astonishing expertise these days to curl a ball beyond the reach of Neville Southall, yet Whiteside managed it with a low shot that was as lethal as an Exocet missile.' Atkinson was now a man constantly looking at his watch and, just as he thought the game might never end, the referee blew his whistle to give Atkinson and United their second FA Cup in three seasons.

The players went to collect the trophy and their medals, except for Moran, who was prohibited from getting a medal, a decision that was rescinded by the FA a few days later. 'I'm going to treat the lads to a drink,' said Moran. 'It's been a traumatic week but I'm delighted it's turned out this way.' The downside after winning the cup was the expulsion of English clubs from European competition following the Heysel disaster in the European Cup Final between Liverpool and Juventus. A wall collapsed, killing 39 people, resulting in a blanket ban for English clubs over the next five seasons.

Without the added pressure of European football, Atkinson's team seemed to thrive as the team kicked off the 1985/86 season by winning their opening ten matches and going 15 unbeaten before losing at Sheffield Wednesday on 9 November. The team had 41 points, double figures ahead of their nearest rivals, and sat on top of the table in February but a mid-season wobble again wrecked their bid for the title. The team only claimed 35 points from their last 27 matches, resulting in a fourth-place finish for the third season in a row. Despite the blistering start, United trailed champions Liverpool by 12 points as the curtain came down on a disappointing end to the campaign.

Not even the solace of the cups could save Atkinson this time as the wheels came off spectacularly after his team led from the front for much of the season. The dip in form coincided with the absence of Bryan Robson, who missed nearly all of the season post-New Year due to injury, proving the earlier point about the missing captain and United's flakiness without their midfield maestro. 'When you are at a club like Man Utd, it's okay winning cups but the fans wanted the league,' said Robson. 'People were getting frustrated, especially after the ten wins on the bounce. People were very frustrated around the club at the end of that year. The pressure was building in the media, too, and the rumours were going about that there might be a change of manager.'

As well as the injury to the captain, a turning point in the season can also be traced back to Atkinson agreeing to the sale of Hughes. The Welsh forward had led United's goalscoring exploits that season but a fee was agreed with Barcelona that spring for him to move at the end of the season. Hughes had scored the majority of his goals before Christmas, barely finding the net in the second half of the season. 'Sparky and I went out for a Christmas drink one day and he told me he was going to Barcelona at the end of the season,' said Whiteside. 'He is the only person that knows if the decision affected him or not, or it could have been a coincidence. Either way, it didn't help the team.'

The highs of 1985 were replaced by the lows of 1986 as the club portrayed its Jekyll and Hyde nature. Whiteside, a hero at Wembley at the end of the previous season, felt frustrated by the team's collapse. 'At the time, too many players were underachieving at the same time and didn't take full responsibility. It was by far our best chance to clinch the title but it just wasn't to be.' It was a sentiment that echoed among the supporters. While the fans yearned for picking the ripest fruit from the tree in regard to winning the First Division title, they were still picking fruit in the cups.

A nightmare start to the 1986/87 season was the last thing that Atkinson needed but a nightmare start he got as his side lost their opening three matches. The team looked a mile away from that of the last couple of years but the boss still had hope that he could turn the tide, despite growing pressure from fans and media. As always, Atkinson spoke like a man who had the enthusiasm of a manager under no pressure at all but his body language spoke a different story.

A New Arrival Brings New Hope

'BIG RON' was finally relieved of his duties on 5 November 1986 with the team languishing near the bottom of the table in 19th position. 'Obviously, I'm a bit disappointed,' said Atkinson. 'Things have gone against us, so I suppose it was inevitable this would eventually happen.' Chairman Martin Edwards had finally pulled the trigger, stating that it was 'in light of the team's poor performance over the last 12 months' and 'in the best interests of club and fans', as he sat and faced the written press.

'I had a good relationship with Ron, though he wasn't quite the character which he portrayed all the time,' Edwards reflected. 'Ron liked exciting football and exciting players. His teams reflected that and he wasn't unsuccessful. He won two FA Cups and we were never out of the top four, which at the time was quite good. It was the league that we were after, though, and we never looked like winning it. We had a great chance in the 1985/86 season when we won the first ten games on the trot but then we started picking up injuries to key players and we didn't have the strength in depth to deal with that.'

As the clock wound down on Atkinson's tenure, the United supremo deemed 'Big Ron' to have fallen below his previously high standards. 'Ron took his eye off the ball a little bit towards the end,' he remarked. 'His marital circumstances probably didn't help … and the results were not coming toward the end; we were near the bottom of the league when he went.' Atkinson had previously offered his resignation but Edwards had waved away his proposition. 'Towards the end of the 85/86 season, he came to me and said "I think I should call it a day this season. I think my time is up". I wasn't sure and told him not to do it, suggesting that he should give it another season.'

It was a decision that just prolonged the inevitable for the club, resulting in another search for a new gaffer. 'What was disappointing, though,' claimed Edwards, 'was that he went to the World Cup in Mexico that summer when I felt he should have been around buying players. He came back and wanted to buy one or two at the last minute, which wasn't ideal preparation.' Atkinson felt that he had unfinished business with the club and was disappointed to be relieved of his duties. 'I'm sad because the things I wanted to do at Old Trafford haven't happened,' he said. 'But I've no complaints. The board have been as supportive as they possibly could and the chairman has been tremendous all the time I have been here.'

Falling attendances and leaks coming out of the club made Atkinson's position almost untenable. The sale of Mark Hughes to Barcelona when United were flying really knocked the wind out of their sails. There was also reportedly a dressing-room bust-up between Jesper Olsen and Remi Moses that somehow found its way into the public domain. With every negative story being circulated, Atkinson's grip on the club loosened to the point where he could no longer keep hold. 'Five of my most productive, essential and senior players – Bryan Robson, Norman Whiteside, Arthur Albiston, Gary Bailey and Gordon Strachan – had returned from the 1986 World Cup to face operations. I believe we have done better than many people have given us credit for and the players are certainly good enough to escape from their present position near the bottom of the table. I'm not bitter. I've had 15 years in football management and this is my first little hiccup.'

Despite Atkinson putting everything into trying to bring success to the club, ultimately he had fallen short of the biggest hurdle of all. 'Big Ron' realised that managing Manchester United was far more demanding than any other club, with the constant media attention and the unrivalled support for both home and away games meaning his every move and decision were scrutinised. The First Division title had become the glazed cherry on the top of a cherry Bakewell in respect that the team were constantly judged on their individual performances, playing the United way, in the hope it would eventually lead to a league championship, but United under Atkinson could be so hot and cold.

Alex Ferguson and Terry Venables had both been sounded out about the position before the club made strides towards the then Aberdeen boss. Ferguson stated: 'United were the only club in the world that could have persuaded me to leave Aberdeen. After eight years working with [Aberdeen chairman] Dick Donald and everybody else at Pittodrie, I cannot begin to express the sadness I feel at having to end what for me has been an unforgettable experience. The Old Trafford job, however, was something I could not turn down.' The deal was done and as quickly as Atkinson departed, Ferguson had arrived, beginning his tenure on 6 November 1986, with Atkinson barely having cleared his desk.

Alex Ferguson was born and raised in Glasgow before forging a career as a footballer in the Scottish League, where he played for Queen's Park, St Johnstone, Dunfermline Athletic, Rangers, Falkirk and Ayr United. Following a successful playing career, Ferguson decided to move into management with East Stirlingshire and quickly gained a reputation for being a disciplinarian. Forward Bobby McCulley later revealed that he had 'never been afraid of anyone before but Ferguson was a frightening bastard from the start'.

Ferguson had taken the reins of the club in the summer of 1974 and found them in the Second Division, the third tier of Scottish football. His stint at Firs Park was short. Just months later, in the October, Ferguson was approached to manage St Mirren, who were also in the Second Division but had a considerably better set-up in regard to stadium and fanbase. It was a decision that took a lot of thought but eventually Ferguson plumped for a move to the Saints.

His first campaign heralded a sixth-place finish but a restructuring of the Scottish League saw St Mirren promoted to the First Division, which was the second tier. Another sixth-place finish was achieved in the 1975/76 season before, a year later, the Saints struck gold with Ferguson, who masterminded a championship-winning season. The team played an attacking brand of football that certainly caught the eye of the locals, with gates swelling from around 1,500 to being in the tens of thousands to see their baby-faced heroes, with the average age of the squad being just over 19. Even the captain, Tony Fitzpatrick, was only 20 when he lifted the First Division trophy. The kids certainly had no fear, that's for sure.

Promotion to the Premier Division had been achieved and against all odds, with relegation a certainty in the eyes of the bookmakers, but St Mirren managed to defy the doubters the following campaign. The Saints finished in a credible eighth place, six points clear of the drop zone and results included a memorable 2-1 win over Celtic as Ferguson showed his team could mix it with the big boys. His young bucks displayed maturity beyond their years to prove they belonged in Scotland's top tier.

The previous summer, Aberdeen had been making noises about bringing Ferguson to Pittodrie but, having just guided St Mirren to success, the manager decided to stay with the Saints as they embarked on a new adventure. Billy McNeill took the vacant position at Aberdeen but the following summer, in 1978, McNeill was offered the chance to take the hotseat at Celtic and he didn't hang around. Aberdeen were again on the lookout and this time Ferguson's ears pricked up. With Aberdeen finishing runners-up in the division, Ferguson saw another chance to climb the ladder.

The Dons had reportedly contacted Ferguson, who was seemingly keen on a switch to the north-east and a job in the third largest city in Scotland. However, his move from St Mirren wasn't as smooth as Ferguson might have anticipated it would be. Having been given the nod for the job by Aberdeen, Ferguson planned his exit from the Saints but there had not been an official approach for his services. Reports claimed that Ferguson had already agreed to leave, including approaching some of his staff and players to come with him, but it was all up in the air until his bosses at St Mirren got wind of what was happening, called Ferguson in for a meeting and terminated his contract with the club.

Willie Todd was the chairman at Love Street and was responsible for eventually pulling the trigger. 'We stayed in the Premier League in season 1977/78 and that was a big achievement,' said Todd when recalling his involvement to *The Guardian*. 'Crowds had been as low as 1,000 when Alex took over; in his last season, we sometimes had gates of 20,000 plus. Alex did a great job for St Mirren. Nobody at the club worked harder than he did during the time he was there and everyone was very grateful for what he achieved. Four days before he eventually left, I knew perfectly well that he had told all the staff that he was moving to Aberdeen.

'A famous reporter of the time, Jim Rodger of the *Daily Mirror*, told us that Alex had asked at least one member of the squad to go to Aberdeen with him. It was a clear breach of contract on his part; he was still under contract to St Mirren and Aberdeen had not contacted us to discuss compensation.' Todd acted in what he thought were the best interests of his club at the time, with Ferguson clearly feeling he had outgrown the Saints by trying to engineer a move to Aberdeen. Despite being sacked, it had the desired outcome for Ferguson and, in June 1978, he was heading to Pittodrie to begin a new life with the Dons.

Aberdeen had won only one Scottish top flight title in their history and that was back in 1955, with the duopoly of Celtic and Rangers claiming the bragging rights in terms of winning league titles, but this did not deter Ferguson from his decision in joining. In fact, he saw it as a challenge. When quizzed about his ambitions for the club, Ferguson set out his pathway. 'Success was winning the League Cup or the FA Cup every six years. The problem was a lot of those players couldn't dream of winning the league,' he said. To go that one step further, he was going to have to install a winning mentality in the dressing room.

'Obviously, I have my own ideas on standards,' said Ferguson 'and, through time, this will come through to the players … fingers crossed.' His maiden campaign heralded a fourth-place finish, as well as a League Cup semi-final and a Scottish Cup Final defeat to his old club, Rangers. It was a defeat that disappointed the manager, with his team not believing that they could actually turn up and win. Ferguson had left Rangers acrimoniously as a player and wanted to exact revenge on a club he felt had turned its back on him. It wasn't to be this time, however, and he would have to bide his time.

'Rather than explain how you can bring a winning mentality to people, you have to produce a project that is working. You have to earn the right to be an Aberdeen player,' said Ferguson. It was a culture that he was trying to bring into the club, changing the mentality of the players when it came down to the big games. Showing up just isn't enough, you have to go out there and prove that you are worthy of being on the same pitch as your opponents and have the mindset that you will find a way to get that result. With Celtic and Rangers at that time, most of the games would have been won in the tunnel, such was the prestige of both clubs.

Gordon Strachan was part of the Aberdeen squad who saw first-hand how committed his boss was to the cause. 'We've all had bollockings off managers at previous clubs but this was an intensity that was not just about that game, it was everything. Where do you want to go? What do you want to do with your life? There is something up here [points to his head] not right, there is something inside this fella that is making him angry and driving him and, looking back, it's like I've bumped into a wounded animal. He put people under so much pressure to be successful. Deep down inside of us, there is a devil that drives us on. For whatever reason, Alex could make that devil materialise for a game of football. He brought the devil out of me.'

Even though that first season ended without any silverware, Ferguson had already begun sowing the seeds of success with his players. 'The first time we played at Rangers, we scrambled a draw in the last minute,' said Ferguson. 'After the game, all the players were celebrating, jumping up and down. And I'm saying "Wait a minute, what you all celebrating for, you've only drawn?"' This was the difference in levels of mentality and the boss worked quickly that summer to ensure the squad was up to the required standards for the start of the 1979/80 season.

The team lost the opening game of the campaign and the fans could have been forgiven for thinking that this was going to be another season of disappointment. Even more so after the club failed to win nine of their first 16 matches but, as the decade changed from the 70s to the 80s,, so did the fortunes of the Dons, who went on a cracking run in the second half of the season, culminating in a draw on the final day of the campaign to lift the Scottish Premier League title. Ferguson's men lost one match out of their final 20 and pipped Celtic by a single point to give Aberdeen only the second league title in their history.

To put into context what an achievement this was, it was the first time in 15 seasons that the league had not been won by either Celtic or Rangers. Defeat to Dundee United meant that it was the second consecutive year the Dons had failed to win at Hampden Park in the Scottish League Cup Final. It scuppered the club's chance of a domestic Double and Ferguson shouldered the blame from the players, saying that he should have made changes to the team for the final. Fast forward a few months, however, and Ferguson's Hampden jinx was about to be lifted at the expense of his old club St Mirren.

Have you ever heard of the Drybrough Cup? Well, it was this little piece of silverware that got the monkey off that Aberdeen team's back. The Drybrough Cup was a competition which had been staged from 1971 until 1974 and was then brought back for one season in 1979/80 before becoming defunct that summer. It consisted of the four highest-scoring teams from the Scottish Premier and the four highest-scoring teams from Division One. The competition was played on a knockout basis with the final held in the week preceding the commencement of the league season.

At that time, the Scottish FA would not allow sponsorship for any of its regular competitions, so the Drybrough brewery got around this regulation by inventing its own tournament and putting its name to it. Aberdeen beat St Mirren 2-1 to lift the trophy prior to the start of the 1980/81 campaign, one that the Dons would start as defending champions. Winning the title put a target on the back of Ferguson and his team and that proved to be the case for Aberdeen that year, with the team finishing second behind Celtic and gaining little to no traction in any of the cup competitions.

A year later and again the Dons were unable to match Celtic in the league, this time falling short by just two points, but it was in the Scottish Cup that Ferguson was about to shape his team's destiny. Facing his nemesis, Rangers, Aberdeen ran out 4-1 winners after a flurry of goals in extra time finally gave Ferguson his retribution in a game that really mattered. More importantly, for both the team and the manager, it meant that the following season Aberdeen would enter the European Cup Winners' Cup.

The Dons had flirted with the European Cup following their title success in 1980 but crashed out early in the competition at the second-round stage, so were looking to make more of a mark this time around as they started another new adventure. They faced Sion, Dinamo Tirana and Lech Poznań in the first three rounds before the draw threw up West German powerhouse Bayern Munich at the quarter-final stage. Aberdeen travelled to the Olympiastadion and returned to Scotland with a tidy 0-0 draw. It looked like a cracking result but Ferguson insisted: 'When we drew 0-0 over there, I was the only one who was unhappy because I thought we needed an away goal and should have got one. We hit the post twice and were the better team.'

With the Dons fancying their chances of progressing, Ferguson sent his team out on a magical night at Pittodrie and saw his side claim an historic 3-2 win over the team from Bavaria. They had to do it the hard way, with the Dons going a goal down in the opening exchanges and again trailing in the second half. But the never-say-die attitude that the boss had instilled in the players shone through on arguably the biggest stage of their footballing careers. Two goals in quick succession turned the match on its head and, just like that, Munich and all of their stars were sent packing.

Waterschei of Belgium lay in wait in the semi-final, with the Dons a fag paper away from reaching a European final. That task looked even more achievable after an imperious 5-1 victory at home to all but seal the deal and virtually ensure a trip to Gothenburg for the final. Even a 0-1 scoreline in the second leg couldn't dampen the mood, as Aberdeen were heading to a European final where they would face none other than arguably Europe's greatest-ever competitors, Real Madrid.

It was a real David v Goliath event, with no one really giving Ferguson's men a chance of defeating Los Blancos, who were managed by their former striker, the legendary Alfredo Di Stéfano. The Dons took the lead through Eric Black after seven minutes but when Juanito equalised from the penalty spot less than ten minutes later, the writing looked to be on the wall for Ferguson and his men. As much as Real Madrid huffed and puffed, though, they couldn't blow down the Aberdeen door and the 90 minutes ended with the score deadlocked at 1-1. So, the game went into extra time and minutes after the restart of the second period, substitute John Hewitt swooped to fire the Dons into a 2-1 lead and into dreamland. The next seven minutes would have felt like an eternity but eventually the referee signalled for full time and Aberdeen of Scotland had beaten Real Madrid of Spain. It was a real giant-killing and one that, quite frankly, no one had seen coming.

The sheer elation spilled out from the players, all of whom had played their part in this crazy cup run. 'The raw energy in that dressing room was frightening,' Gordon Strachan recalled in the 2013 book *Glory in Gothenburg*. 'If you could have turned that into electricity, you could have powered the whole of the north of Scotland.'

Goalscoring hero Hewitt had been a ballboy at Pittodrie growing up, so to score the winning goal in a European final would have meant as much to him as anyone else in that side. He told BBC Scotland: 'Once we knocked out Bayern – I came on as a sub to score the winner – we were the best team in the competition. That's what Alex Ferguson said and I think he was right. They were basically the German national team. We beat Waterschei in the semi-final to set up the final with Real Madrid. People say "Oh, the mighty Real Madrid", but that was the thing about us, we never feared anybody.'

Hewitt looked back with fondness on his role in the win but laughed when he remembered the antics his boss would get up to, which included a fine system for nearly everything. These were just some of the ways that Ferguson tried to build a camaraderie amongst the group, ensuring that he had a strong dressing room to work with. 'Everybody had a fine from Alex at some point. Even for the slightest things – you were in the treatment room without his permission, you got fined. He used to love fining you for anything he could.

'The classic was when we were training in the winter … we were on the way back from the gym and the roads were clear but it had been snowing. I had a car full of players. He was in front of me in his Mercedes doing about 10mph. I was egged on to overtake him, which I did. The guys were hanging out the window, waving, which infuriated him. Within 30 seconds of getting back, he burst into the dressing room, hurling abuse at me. The following week, I saw I had a £20 fine in my wages and that was it.'

Aberdeen really enjoyed playing their role as the underdogs and Ferguson described the win as 'nothing short of a miracle'. He even used an old trick he'd learned from Jock Stein by presenting his opposite number, Di Stéfano, with a bottle of whisky to give the impression that he and his team were just happy to be part of the occasion. 'Let him feel important,' Stein told him. 'As if you are thrilled just to be in the final.'

Ferguson's team battled hard on four fronts that season and, despite crashing out of the League Cup, looked to be heading towards a second league title in three seasons. The problem was, Dundee United just kept on winning. Aberdeen finished third in a three-horse race, finishing joint second with Celtic on goal difference and only a point behind champions Dundee United. It was oh so close for the Dons, who missed out on another title by a whisker but, just a week later, they managed to retain the Scottish Cup with another extra time win over Rangers, having dispatched Celtic in the semi-final.

After not being able to win at Hampden Park, suddenly the team couldn't lose in the national stadium. Yet, while the players were sat celebrating post-match, little did they know that their boss was tearing them apart on national television. Considering the jubilation of the Cup Winners' Cup and demands of the final stages of the league campaign, it was no wonder those players had looked a little leggy at Hampden. They had, nonetheless, won – but that was not enough for the boss, who went on a rant in his post-match interview.

'A disgrace of a performance,' he raged, sparing only two players from the tirade, his two trusty centre-backs. '[Willie] Miller and [Alex] McLeish played Rangers by themselves. Winning cups doesn't matter. Our standards have been set long ago and I'm not going to accept that from any Aberdeen team.' Such was the demeanour of the boss during the celebratory meal that it was reported the atmosphere resembled more of a wake than a cup victory celebration. Gordon Strachan had apparently refused to even attend the event, such was his disdain over Ferguson's outburst, one which he later apologised for.

Eric Black, who was by now becoming a bit of a cup final specialist after his run of goals in showpieces, remembered a carnival atmosphere in the changing room … 'Then, all of a sudden, the door went screaming open

– and it was like the sheriff coming into the saloon bar in the Wild West. The door was rattling on its hinges and he just went ballistic at us. That put a bit of a dampener on everything.'

Despite that cup final performance, Aberdeen were on a crest of a wave as they began the 1983/84 season. They claimed another Premier Division title, Scottish Cup and even managed to beat the European Cup winners Hamburg in the European Super Cup Final. After a 0-0 draw in the first leg, the Dons again lifted European silverware following a 2-0 win at Pittodrie. It was another successful campaign that saw the club's second top-flight title in five years, as well a hat-trick of Scottish Cup Final wins being secured.

The following year, the Dons secured back-to-back league titles as Ferguson's men were once again the cream of the crop in Scotland, despite crashing out of all the cup competitions. Even a first-round exit from the European Cup couldn't dampen the mood around Pittodrie as Aberdeen continued to upset the establishment by breaking the Old Firm stranglehold. Ferguson achieved his latest success in spite of losing one of his star players, Gordon Strachan, who was sold to Manchester United for around £500,000.

In the 1985/86 season, too many draws were the undoing of the Dons and they could only muster a fourth-place finish. Despite the downturn in league form, they managed to secure both domestic cups.

Both finals were won by 3-0 margins, with Hearts and Hibernian defeated in the Scottish Cup and League Cup, respectively. That summer in Mexico, Ferguson took the helm of the Scottish national team following the death of Jock Stein but was unable to guide the side out of the group stages. It was both disappointing and emotional, as Stein had been a mentor for Ferguson and his sudden passing had left a hole. But that was about to be filled by a brand new challenge. Ferguson started the 1986/87 season with Aberdeen but, just four months later, the call came from Manchester United and, just like that, his time in his native Scotland was over.

'Manchester United are the only club I would have left Aberdeen to join,' he told the *Daily Mirror*. 'I'm looking forward to a tremendous challenge. Everything has happened so fast that I'm slightly bewildered. I recall the late Jock Stein once telling me that the biggest mistake he made was to turn down the Manchester United job and I made sure that I wouldn't do the same. But it will be a great wrench to leave Aberdeen.' Ferguson didn't leave alone, bringing his assistant, Archie Knox, with him. The pair had worked together at Pittodrie and for the national team, so having his right-hand man with him was ideal for the manager as he looked to settle in his new surroundings.

Ferguson moved south and was thrust straight into his new job, with a game to prepare for just 48 hours later, away to Oxford United. The boss was reuniting with one of his former charges, Strachan, who quipped to his team-mates: 'I never thought he'd follow me this far south!' His first United team lined up at the Manor Ground that day like this: Turner; Duxbury, Moran, Hogg, Albiston; Moses, McGrath, Blackmore; Barnes, Davenport, Stapleton. A 2-0 defeat was a sobering welcome for Ferguson, who would have to work fast to drag the team away from the foot of the table.

In his post-match press conference, Ferguson was in bullish mood. 'I'm glad it's over,' he said. 'It was a nightmare trying to concentrate with so much media attention and so many cameramen on top of me. I was disappointed with the atmosphere. I expected it to be more like a cup tie but perhaps supporters in Scotland are more vociferous. The players' confidence has taken a bit of a battering. We only played with any composure when we went 2-0 down. You could see the strain come off the players and maybe that was understandable. They were a bit uptight and they wanted to do well.' His principles and philosophy would be identical to that he had with Aberdeen.

Despite his less-than-ideal start to the tenure at his new club, there was still a positive outlook on the new appointment at Old Trafford. Patrick Glenn, reporting for *The Observer*, wrote: 'When Martin Edwards offered Alex Ferguson the Manchester United job last Thursday, it was as if the Big Fisherman himself had held out the key to the Pearly Gates.

The very idea of Ferguson's non-acceptance was absurd. His irresistible competitiveness – at times, it borders on the psychopathic – has long been sustained by apparently endless energy and to have refused the biggest club in Britain would have seemed to Ferguson a self-betrayal deserving of hara-kiri. Ferguson's unshakable commitment to whatever cause he espouses has been evident since, as a teenager, he led his fellow apprentice toolmakers' industrial action at their factory on the south side of Glasgow.'

A 0-0 draw away to Norwich City was played out a week later before Ferguson finally got off the mark at Old Trafford with a 1-0 win over Queens Park Rangers. A crowd of 42,235 witnessed a John Sivebæk goal and the third highest gate of the campaign so far, as Ferguson marked his first home match with three vital points. In fact, United's form from then on in seemed to improve and included, most notably, a cracking 1-0 win at Anfield on Boxing Day, upsetting title challengers Liverpool. This was followed by a 4-1 demolition of Newcastle United on the first day of 1987 as the Red Devils began a nine-match unbeaten run.

Only a handful of defeats in the second half of the season could dampen the mood as the team climbed the First Division table, eventually securing an 11th-place finish. It was certainly considered to be progress but it was really only to be expected, such was the quality of players at the manager's disposal. Ferguson had only made one signing in the seven months he had been in charge, a 14-year-old called Alan Tongue, with the manager clearly wanting to evaluate his squad. His team were going to have to work hard and be disciplined in both their professional roles and their lifestyles, with reports circulating that there was a renowned drinking culture at the club, something that goalkeeper Gary Bailey later admitted was a concern.

In an article for *TNT Sports*, written by the well-respected Manchester United fanzine *United We Stand* creator, Andy Mitten, Bailey was quick to dismiss the antics of his team-mates. 'The drinking culture was a problem, no question,' recalled United's man between the sticks. 'It wasn't a problem for people like Bryan Robson, who enjoyed the drinking and still performed perfectly well. But it created a culture that other players were not comfortable with. I believe in looking after your body, watching what you eat and being physiologically stable. I bumped heads constantly with the "You cope or piss off home approach".'

Ferguson began to ring the changes in the summer of 1987 when Martin Edwards opened the cheque book and allowed the manager to bring in both Viv Anderson from Arsenal and Brian McClair from Celtic for a combined fee of around £1.5m. This was followed just a few months later with another £1m-plus splash for Norwich City defender Steve Bruce. The new recruits seemed to settle in quickly as, by the end of August,

United sat top of the pile. Too many draws again hindered efforts to stay at the summit, with Ferguson's men struggling to get maximum points on far too many occasions while Liverpool, who had by now overtaken United at the top, would go on to lose only two games all season.

One of the highlights of the campaign was the 3-3 draw with Liverpool at Anfield on 4 April 1988 during the Easter weekend programme. United were trailing their rivals by 12 points and a defeat would hand Liverpool the title in front of their own fans. 'Captain Marvel' Bryan Robson opened the scoring after just three minutes when a cross from Peter Davenport was turned in past Bruce Grobbelaar. Eight minutes before half-time and the hosts drew level through Peter Beardsley. In the blink of an eye, Liverpool took a 2-1 lead, Beardsley turning provider this time for Gary Gillespie to head home.

Just two minutes after the restart and Liverpool scored again with a long-range piledriver from Steve McMahon. That was surely it now, with the champions elect running riot and United losing their heads when a calm approach was the order of the day. On the hour, Colin Gibson was given his second yellow card of the day and an already uphill task was now bordering on the impossible. Six minutes later and the travelling support had reason to believe when a deflected Robson shot bewitched Grobbelaar to bring the deficit back to one. Ferguson screamed at his players to race back into position so that the game could be restarted. The manager smelt blood. He still believed that there could be a result here.

With just over ten minutes remaining, the comeback was complete as one of Ferguson's trusty lieutenants nabbed an equaliser. Davenport was again the man with the assist as he controlled the ball, span and played a beautiful, chipped pass between Liverpool's rearguard and into the path of the onrushing Strachan, who fired low past Grobbelaar to level the match at 3-3. The midfielder wheeled off towards the Kop and brought out the iconic 'cigar' celebration; for those readers of an older generation, you will know exactly what I mean.

The Times' Martin Searby was fully justified when opening his match report with these words: 'It would be difficult to conceive of a game more filled with passion, pace, skill and commitment than that provided by the two sides at the top of the First Division at Anfield yesterday.' Despite his team's impressive turnaround, Ferguson was furious heading into his post-match media duties. 'I can now understand why teams come away from here choking on their own vomit and biting their tongues knowing they have been done by the referee,' Ferguson commented. 'I'm not getting at this referee. The whole intimidating atmosphere and the monopoly Liverpool have enjoyed for years gets to them eventually.'

Ferguson had witnessed first-hand the sheer relentlessness that Liverpool possessed as his team battled hard at the top of the table but were unable to cut away at Liverpool's eventual nine-point lead. United had, in fact, only lost twice since Boxing Day, winning seven of their last eight matches, but the damage had already been done in the autumn of the campaign when draws curtailed an early title charge, with United having to settle for just one point on eight occasions in the opening 15 fixtures. Following the festive period, the team seemed to click into gear but it was too little, too late.

In Ferguson's short time in England, Liverpool – having already won the Charity Shield before his arrival – had won the First Division title and finished as runners-up in both the FA Cup and League Cup. They had, of course, won countless league titles, European Cups, League Cups and FA Cups over the previous 15-year period. It was a conveyor belt of trophies that had passed through the gates at Anfield but that did not deter Ferguson. If anything, it made the job in hand seem even more appetising. 'This isn't just a job to me. It's a mission,' said Ferguson. 'I am deadly serious about it – some people would reckon too serious. We will get there and, believe me, when it happens, life will change for Liverpool and everybody else – dramatically.' A bold statement, indeed.

It wasn't all doom and gloom at Old Trafford, though, as the positives started to outweigh the negatives. A decent league record of only four defeats all season, with only one coming on home soil, was enough to give both the manager and the fans optimism for the future. A second-place finish inspired by the deadly finishing of new signing Brian McClair had signalled another new dawn in Manchester. McClair scored 24 league goals that campaign, the first time any United player had scored more than 20 since George Best back in the 1967/68 season.

As the season drew to a close, Ferguson broke the record for the highest fee paid for a Youth Training Scheme (YTS) player when he spent around £200,000 on Lee Sharpe, a 16-year-old winger from Torquay United. And the spending didn't stop there. Clearly the second-place finish in the table excited Martin Edwards, as yet again the chairman parted with his cash, this time to the tune of around £3.5m. Fans' favourite Mark Hughes was resigned from Barcelona, upping the levels of excitement even further amongst the supporters.

Mal Donaghy was brought in from Luton Town, Ralph Milne from Bristol City and Jim Leighton – Ferguson's No.1 at Pittodrie – from Aberdeen as the manager began to put together the pieces of his Manchester United puzzle ahead of the 1988/89 season. The Scot thought he had sealed the deal on a young midfielder from Newcastle United called Paul Gascoigne, but 'Gazza' went back on his word with the manager while Ferguson was away on holiday, instead plumping for a lucrative move to London with Tottenham Hotspur. 'Can I go on holiday, knowing that I've signed you Gazza?' asked Ferguson. 'Go and enjoy yourself Mr Ferguson, I'll be signing for Manchester United,' insisted Gazza. He never made it to Old Trafford, instead opting for the bright lights of the capital.

The team struggled to find any rhythm and were inconsistent from the outset, a trait that had followed the club all the way through the 1980s. As with the previous season, draws were the Achilles' heel for Ferguson's side, drawing nine of their first 14 matches. This struggle for form left United in tenth position as the Red Devils reached the festive period. Many believed that a 3-1 win over champions Liverpool on New Year's Day would be the catalyst for a title charge in the second half of the campaign. Wins throughout January and February did catapult the team into third place before another collapse in form scuppered any chance of a championship push. It wasn't to be as the team failed to build on the momentum, eventually finishing in a disappointing 11th place.

Mark Hughes had returned to lead the goalscoring for the team with joint top goalscorer Brian McClair, as well as collecting the PFA Players' Player of the Year award. Jim Leighton had only conceded 35 goals in 38 matches, keeping 15 clean sheets, but it was the inability to turn draws into wins that eventually hamstrung the team. The finale of the season also saw some big names depart the club, with Gordon Strachan heading across the Pennines to rivals Leeds United while Norman Whiteside and Paul McGrath were allowed to leave for Everton and Aston Villa, respectively.

It was a bold move from the manager but one that he felt he had good reason for. 'Strachan was never the same player that he was at Aberdeen,' said Ferguson. 'It was controversial and quite astonishing to some of the supporters, as these were tremendously talented players, and I've gone on record before to say how great a player I think Whiteside is. He should go for another challenge somewhere. I think he would be the first to agree that it's the right thing to do. And then you have Paul. I couldn't accept the way he wants to live his life and that's about it, really. At the end of the day, you stand and fall by your decisions. I think management is about making decisions and being positive about making decisions. People recognise positive behaviours in managers and players look at you and think "Oof! This man means business".'

So, with two 11th-place finishes and a runners-up spot during a two-and-a-half-season spell in charge, had there really been any progress made or were the club in the status quo scenario that Ron Atkinson had them in? The following year was going to be pivotal to Ferguson at Manchester United … and he didn't even know it yet.

The 1989/90 Campaign – A Knighton Shining Armour?

The Squad:

Goalkeepers – Jim Leighton, Gary Walsh, Mark Bosnich, Les Sealey*

Defenders – Viv Anderson, Clayton Blackmore, Mal Donaghy, Mike Duxbury, Colin Gibson, Lee Martin, Derek Brazil, Gary Pallister**

Midfielders – Russell Beardsmore, Deiniol Graham, Paul Ince***, Ralph Milne, Mike Phelan****, Bryan Robson, Lee Sharpe, Neil Webb****

Forwards – Mark Hughes, Giuliano Maiorana, Brian McClair, Mark Robins, Danny Wallace*****

* – On Loan from December

** – Signed in August

*** – Signed in September

**** – Signed in July

PREPARING FOR a new season is a difficult enough task to navigate as it is but, with rumours of a takeover at the club in the offing, Ferguson was going to have to find a way to block out the noise. Martin Edwards had decided to shake hands on a £20m deal to sell the club with property tycoon businessman and football fan Michael Knighton. Edwards had only been chairman for just under ten years following the death of his father, Louis, but decided that he wanted to part company with the club. 'I believe that under new direction and with new financial backing this club can go even further,' Edwards said after agreeing to the sale. The deal was initially thought to be split into two stages, with £10m paid to Edwards for a 50.06 per cent controlling stake, followed by a further investment of £10m towards upgrading both the playing staff and the iconic Stretford End.

Knighton was convinced that he could escalate United's annual turnover of £7m and bolster both the commercial revenue and the playing side of things. He knew that a successful club would, in turn, bring results with a successful team on the pitch. 'We shall tap into every conceivable market,' claimed Knighton as he batted away the critics who were using the press as a weapon against his proposed plans. Reflecting later on the scepticism surrounding his takeover plan, he said: 'It seemed obvious to me to get hold of one of the greatest brands in the sector would be like owning a goldmine but, at the time, I was pretty much alone in that view. The *Financial Times* asked me why I was buying a club that had just announced a loss of £1.3m and was only turning over £7m a year. I said I was buying potential, that I thought it should be possible to turn United into the world's wealthiest club.'

The takeover news couldn't have come at a worse time for Ferguson, published just three days before the start of the 1989/90 campaign. Despite the uncertainty surrounding the financial side of the deal, Edwards still allowed Ferguson to push on with his summer spending. Mike Phelan and Neil Webb were signed from Norwich City and Nottingham Forest, respectively, for a combined fee of around £2.25m but fan favourite Norman Whiteside was sold to Everton as the manager looked to freshen up his midfield. 'When the manager sold Paul McGrath and Norman Whiteside, he was getting rid of big fans' favourites and it was a really big decision,' recalls Bryan Robson. 'A lot has been said about the manager not being happy with their lifestyle but I think the major factor with both Norman and Paul was their injuries and the manager felt he couldn't rely on their fitness anymore. But when you move players on who are popular with the supporters, you have to get results to justify your decision.'

It was another bold statement from a manager who was going to need a great start to the season to subdue the negativity that was building from the previous year.

There could be no more excuses. This was now starting to become his team, with him now shaping the squad his way. 'You could see the changes being made by the manager and how they were improving the club,' said Robson. 'He had brought in good, solid characters like Brian McClair, re-signed Mark Hughes from Barcelona and changed how we trained, how we ate and instilled more discipline throughout the club. We could all see how he was changing things on the youth development side of the club but it did take time to turn it around.' And, as we all know, time is not on a manager's side when results are not going their way.

The opening day of the season saw the visit of the league champions Arsenal, as well as the much talked about pre-match entertainment from the club's new owner. Knighton, dressed in full training kit, did keepie-uppies in front of a packed Stretford End before slamming the ball into an empty net, which was met with a huge cheer from the inquisitive crowd. 'Many grown men dream of emulating George Best and scoring at the Stretford End. But to try it in front of a packed ground was the act of a brave man,' a local news reporter stated at the time. 'The new chairman could have fallen flat on his face in every sense but, in a few minutes of pure indulgence, he did what his predecessor didn't manage in eight years – he won over one of the country's most critical crowds.' Knighton enjoyed the public show of affection. 'I wanted to show the fans I was one of them, a football fan first and a businessman second. I was there because I wanted to make a difference,' he told *MEN Sport*.

You could have been excused for thinking this could have backfired on United, with this charade taking place moments before the opening stages of a new First Division campaign, but maybe it was just the tonic the players and supporters needed heading into a new season. Some good news to give the place the feelgood factor. Ferguson sent his team out with Jim Leighton in goal, Donaghy, Duxbury, Bruce and Blackmore in defence. The midfield consisted of new signings Webb and Phelan, as well as Robson and Sharpe, supporting McClair and Hughes up top.

The season couldn't have got off to a better start, with Steve Bruce swooping low to head in a Lee Sharpe corner after just two minutes, and it could have been even better moments later, only for McClair to see his tame spot kick saved by John Lukic, diving low to his left. It was a rallying call for the champions of England who equalised through David Rocastle midway through the first half following a corner of their own. United led again just after the hour when an excellent turn from Hughes saw the Welshman fire low and through the legs of Lukic.

United's football was nearly as bright as the Manchester summer sun and when new boy Webb scored on his debut, it looked to be the cherry on the cake for Ferguson and his men. The England international's fantastic volley from the corner of the 18-yard box was the pick of the bunch, fizzing past the hapless Lukic, who could only wave it past. McClair rounded off the scoring with a curling left-footed effort into the far corner after some fortunate ricochets had gone his way. When it's your day, it's your day.

A 4-1 win against a team that would be there or thereabouts in the title race was a fantastic way to start but that's all it was at this stage, a start. Even what some deemed to be a circus prior to kick-off hadn't knocked Ferguson's men out of their stride, including the beaming Webb. 'We had heard about the takeover but this chap came into the dressing room before the game, introduced himself as the new owner and then asked for a kit,' Webb later recalled. 'We thought he just wanted to join in with the warm-up but I couldn't believe what I was seeing when he ran on to the pitch and whacked the ball into the net at the Stretford End. It was hilarious, really. Unbelievable.'

United legend George Best was excited about the winds of change that were about to sweep through the club. 'I think sometimes when a new face comes in, no matter at what level, it has a good effect on a club,' he told the BBC's *Grandstand* sports show. 'I hope it is going to be the same at Manchester United.' But others were still not quite convinced about the club's proposed new owner. 'He's had to provide £20m for this takeover, so presumably he has had to borrow a great deal of that, which means he'll have heavy interest to cover,' the *Manchester Evening News'* legendary former chief United writer, David Meek, warned on *Grandstand*. 'It means he'll want a dividend on his shares from Manchester United, which means that the club must make a profit in order to pay a dividend. So, I don't see that they can buy a lot of expensive players and pay a dividend to Mr Knighton. So, really, not a lot has changed.'

Ferguson kept faith with the same starting XI three days later when the team travelled to Selhurst Park to take on Crystal Palace. Bryan Robson fired a low right-footed shot past Nigel Martyn to give the visitors the lead on 19 minutes. It looked like the solitary goal was going to be enough to seal three points on the road before Ian Wright's injury-time equaliser meant that United would have to get back on the bus with just the one point but still sitting pretty at the top of the table, with four points from a possible six. Ferguson's men were on the road again the following weekend, this time heading to the Baseball Ground to take on Derby County, with the manager making only one change to his starting XI as Lee Martin made his first start of the season, replacing Mal Donaghy in the defence. Goals from Paul Goddard and a late penalty from Dean Sturridge were enough to hand Ferguson and his men their first defeat of the season.

Off the field, it was reported in the press that the takeover of the club was gathering pace but that Knighton was not a lone wolf in his bid to acquire the majority of shares that would eventually lead to a full purchase from Martin Edwards. In fact, it was said that Knighton wasn't even the man with the money. 'Bob Thornton is, indeed, a partner in my MK Trafford Holdings [the company set up by Knighton for the takeover]. He's my dear friend and everyone knows he's an outstanding and exceptional businessman and former leader of a major retail unit in Debenhams PLC. Bob and I know and understand each other very well,' said Knighton when quizzed about his financial clout.

Following the defeat at Derby, Ferguson made a plea to the board to bolster his squad even further with the acquisition of central defender Gary Pallister from Middlesbrough for a British record fee of around £2.3m, taking the club's summer spending to roughly £4.5m. Now, you have to remember that this was over half of the previous season's turnover, so to spend that amount the following summer was a big gamble from those holding the purse strings. Despite the grumblings that had been reverberating around the place over the last six to 12 months, the manager clearly had the full backing of the board.

Record signing Pallister was seen as an excellent addition to the squad, despite the huge price tag. 'Yes, there was a lot of press talk about it after it went through,' said Pallister. 'I would never say I was worth £2.3m but, if you see the likes of Paul Gascoigne or Tony Cottee, they would say the same. That's the way the market's going at the moment. Clubs are asking for ridiculous fees at the moment but, thankfully, Middlesbrough didn't overprice me too much and, thankfully, Manchester United came in and paid the money and I eventually got here.'

Pallister was thrust straight into the side at the expense of Lee Martin, who was dropped to the bench for the visit of Norwich City to Old Trafford, giving the Stretford End a glimpse of their new signing. Dale Gordon opened the scoring for the Canaries moments before half-time before debutant Pallister had a moment to forget when he flattened Robert Rosario in the area, gifting Robert Fleck a chance to double the score from the penalty spot, which he gratefully accepted. A 2-0 defeat at home meant that it was now only one win in four and that United had gone two matches without even finding the net. Norwich's local newspaper, the *Eastern Daily Press*, mocked United with the headline: 'Cut price Canaries give the rich kids a hiding.'

The national press began to reach for their pitchforks, too. 'After the sunny start it was back to the grey days,' wrote Clive White in *The Times*. 'Losing their next match, 2-0 at home to Norwich, did not help Ferguson's case.' With £2.3m signing Pallister giving away a penalty on his debut and influential skipper Robson limping out, the 'Woe upon woe for United' headline in *The Times* was spot on. When Webb ruptured his Achilles tendon while on international duty, Ferguson must have been bemoaning his luck.

In a bid to change fortunes on the pitch, Ferguson fielded six defenders in a side that was now missing the heart of its midfield, with both Webb and Robson in the treatment room. Donaghy came into the starting XI, as well as Lee Martin, with Duxbury and Blackmore pushing into the midfield. Despite the defensive look to the team, United still managed to ship three goals in a 3-2 defeat at Goodison Park to an Everton team who had started the season in fine fettle.

There was now a gaping hole in the Manchester United midfield that needed plugging and Ferguson had been alerted to the potential of West Ham United midfielder Paul Ince, who had been ripping it up at Upton Park the previous season despite his team suffering relegation to the second tier. A lot of clubs were sniffing around the midfielder, so United wasted no time in splashing out £1m to bring him to Old Trafford. Ince played just once in the Second Division for the Hammers that season before completing a highly controversial transfer to the Red Devils, with the fans of his former club less than impressed over the midfielder's antics.

Ince had been photographed in a Manchester United kit long before the transfer was complete and when the picture appeared in the *Daily Express*, it led to the midfielder receiving plenty of abuse from West Ham fans, many of whom felt the deal and the way Ince went about it was quite underhanded. The initial move was postponed after he failed a medical but was quickly revisited and completed on 14 September 1989 after he later received the all-clear. It was the end of a drawn-out saga and one that Ince still gets hate from today. In an article in *FourFourTwo* magazine, he said:

'I spoke to Alex Ferguson and the deal was close to being done. I then went on holiday and my agent at the time, Ambrose Mendy, said it wasn't worth me coming back to do a picture in a United shirt when the deal was completed, so I should do one before I left and it would be released when the deal was announced. Lawrence Lustig of the *Daily Star* took the picture and put it in the library. Soon after, their sister paper, the *Daily Express,* were looking for a picture of me playing for West Ham and found the one of me in the United shirt in the pile. They published it and all hell broke loose. I came back from holiday to discover West Ham fans were going mad. It wasn't really my fault. I was only a kid. I did what my agent told me to do, then took all the crap for it.'

Following the defeat to the Toffees, United found themselves in 16th position and, after what seemed like a promising start to the campaign, quickly found it unravelling at a rapid rate of knots. The results, bar the opening couple of fixtures, seemed to have carried on from the tail end of the previous season, when seven defeats in 11 matches condemned Ferguson's men to the obscurity of mid-table. Now, though, this was starting to be considered Ferguson's side, with many fresh faces being added to the squad.

New signing Ince slotted straight into midfield with Phelan, Sharpe and skipper Bryan Robson, who made a welcome return from injury, for the visit of Millwall to Old Trafford. Sitting in the stands that day was yet another new signing, with Ferguson bringing in Danny Wallace from Southampton for around £1.2m. The diminutive winger had electric pace and had earned rave reviews down at The Dell, adding extra trickery and distribution alongside the youthful Sharpe.

Mark Hughes was in imperious form that day as the forward netted a hat-trick in a 5-1 demolition of the Lions to stop a run of defeats, with the football as bright as the Manchester sunshine. The pick of the bunch was the opening goal and Hughes's first. A long kick upfield was plucked out of the sky by the Welshman, who then rolled his marker before taking a touch and driving his shot into the far top-right corner. Robson scored United's second goal after some neat build-up play down the left found the midfielder in space on the edge of the box to curl his effort into the far corner.

Speaking to the press after the game, Hughes said: 'Yeah, it went particularly well for myself and for the team as well. We felt that, leading up to this game, we hadn't been playing that badly, we just haven't had the breaks, really, but today we had the breaks and it was a good performance all-round.' A midweek trip to Fratton Park to take on Portsmouth in the Littlewoods Cup (League Cup) saw goals from two of the team's newest stars, with Ince grabbing a brace and Wallace notching in a 3-2 victory.

Amidst the break from the league campaign, takeover talks seemed to be gathering more momentum as the proposed end date edged ever closer. Martin Edwards had mixed emotions over the deal that would see his family finally relinquish control of a club they had owned for many years. 'Well, I have got many mixed feelings, obviously,' said Edwards. 'In one sense it's very sad. I have been the chairman here for ten years now and it's a big wrench to give that up but the reasons I did the deal in the first place still stand, with Michael Knighton willing to back the build of the new Stretford End with £10m and that was something I felt was a long way down the road had I remained in the chair. So, yes, very mixed feelings, really.'

The date 23 September 1989 is etched into the memory of Reds of a certain age. United headed off to Maine Road for a derby match that turned out to be a pretty awful day at the office, with Hughes's scissor-kick volley the only highlight in a 5-1 mauling from the hosts. City had just been promoted from the Second

Division and had only one win to their name until this Maine Road massacre upset the red half of the city. It was arguably Ferguson's darkest hour as Manchester United manager and one that us supporters would struggle to ever forget. Goal after goal hit Jim Leighton's net as City ran riot against a United team who failed to muster barely any kind of retaliation. It was another chink in the manager's armour as he continued his quest to appease the growing unrest amongst supporters. Of the City defeat, Ferguson said: 'I remember after the game, I got home and I just stayed in my bed. Probably the best place to be.'

But it wasn't only the locals that were getting restless after the team's poor start to the season, the press were sharpening their knives as well. As the calendar ticked into October, already the wolves were at the door for the boss, who was quick to knock back any talk of a crisis. 'I don't think it's personal,' said Ferguson. 'I just think it's because I'm the manager of Manchester United and I think that managers of Manchester United have always been the whipping boys for the press. They have nothing to write about and a story about Manchester United will sell them papers. I think it's a lot to do with that.' The red tops were having a field day with their back page headlines. 'From boardroom to dressing room, United are showing all the classic signs of a club cracking up,' wrote Harry Harris in the *Daily Mirror*.

Record signing Pallister had been at the forefront of the abuse from the supporters following the team's diabolical display in the derby. It was a steep learning curve for the former Middlesbrough defender, who was finding out what it really meant to represent Manchester United. Such defeats, especially to your city rivals, were not going to be tolerated. There is a standard that must be adhered to, demanded not only by the club and coaching staff but also the supporters. Pallister recalled being confronted by 'four burly United fans' when he reported for training on the Monday morning. 'They told me I wasn't fit to wear a United shirt, [that] we shouldn't have sold Paul McGrath, [that] I was a "disgrace" to the club,' he recalled. 'They really ripped into us and it was quite frightening.'

But despite all this, the club kept faith with Ferguson, even offering him a new contract until the end of the 1992/93 season, which he duly accepted. If United thought the outside noise about performances on the pitch was loud, it was about to get a whole lot louder over events off it as the proposed takeover with Knighton hit the rocks. In mid-September, fellow investors Bob Thornton and Stanley Cohen pulled out of the deal, leaving Knighton searching for further investment if he were to make his dream of owning United a reality. Other financiers were approached to join him on his proposed venture, with Knighton proving to chairman

Edwards and his legal team that he did, indeed, have the funds to complete the initial deal.

Amid the looming deadline for a deal to be completed, further scrutiny regarding the financing of the initial investment, as well as cynicism regarding the lofty global ambitions he had for the club, led Knighton to hand back the contract he had agreed with Edwards. By mid-October, all talks of a takeover were off as Knighton accepted a non-executive role on the board of directors and eventually watched on as United fulfilled his predictions as a mass marketing machine, leaving the proposed buyer with only a seat at the table and proverbial egg on his face.

'I'm known as "the man who tried to buy Manchester United but didn't have the money",' he told the *Daily Mirror*. 'But that's absolute rubbish. I had the cash all right – and I also had a £24m overdraft facility to back it up. In fact, when Martin Edwards told me he wanted £10m for his shares, I almost fell off my chair because I was ready to pay four times as much.' Knighton believed he held the key that would open up United into a commercial monster, much like what you see today. At that time, football clubs were still run as the name suggested, clubs, not as the businesses they have now become. Knighton might well have given Edwards the nudge he needed to fully realise the potential United held – not just in Old Trafford on matchdays, or in Manchester itself, but on a global scale.

'I gave Martin my blueprint after we aborted the deal,' says Knighton. 'He was incredibly tolerant of me because he must have thought I was a raving lunatic. I said I was going to turn the club into a £150m leisure vehicle that would make profits so large we could buy any player in the world. He told me we were turning over £7m and the club hadn't made money for 20 years and had just announced £1.3m losses. I told him it would happen. At that time, hardly anyone thought satellite TV would replace terrestrial. I said it would transform football.'

Some supporters accused the players of hiding behind the excuse of the takeover saga, an accusation that was refuted by skipper Robson. A 0-0 draw at home to Sheffield Wednesday on 14 October 1989 did little to lighten the mood before a 4-1 win at Highfield Road over Coventry City moved United up three places in the table to 14th. Goals from Bruce and Phelan, plus a brace from Hughes were enough to take the three points back to Old Trafford, ensuring the team's first win on the road. High-scoring Southampton were the next visitors in M16 and were swiftly sent packing back down the M1 empty-handed following a 2-1 victory courtesy of two Brian McClair goals.

October ended in a whimper with a 3-0 defeat to Tottenham Hotspur in the Littlewoods Cup and the beginning of November continued in the same vein as a 2-0 away defeat at the hands of Charlton Athletic saw

United seesaw back into 13th position. Not even Guy Fawkes could ignite United's attack as the Red Devils again drew a blank, their sixth in all competitions already that season. Ferguson refused to talk to the press after his side suffered another defeat, with the media rounding on the manager on his third anniversary at the club. The *Daily Express* went with the headline 'Fergie the flop' and Colin Gibson was scathing in the *Daily Telegraph*. 'They [the supporters] are fed up with excuses and false dawns. Old Trafford needs success and it needs it quickly, otherwise the pressure Mr Ferguson has experienced will grow much worse.'

As the nights began to draw in, the skies around Ferguson were seemingly becoming darker with every passing day.

FA Cup Third Round – Chopping Down the Forest

Venue: The City Ground
Date: 7 January 1990
Attendance: 23,072

THERE'S SOMETHING quite magical about going to the football on a Saturday afternoon once the clocks have changed at the end of October. Floodlights come on around half-time as the skies blacken with every passing minute. The smell of Bovril begins to fill the autumn air as spectators use any means necessary to stay warm. Manchester, more often than not, due to its abhorrent weather patterns, tends to see this slightly earlier than most of the country. While you may be thinking 'why on earth are we getting a weather rundown here' and while I digress, the scene I am setting not only filled the Manchester skies but also the mood around Old Trafford at that time.

On 12 November, United welcomed the TV cameras to Old Trafford as *The Big Match Live* came to town for the visit of Nottingham Forest in a First Division match. A crowd of just over 34,000 turned out to see a team consisting of Leighton, Blackmore, Martin, Bruce, Pallister, Phelan, Ince, Robson, Wallace, Hughes and McClair bid to get the Red Devils back to winning ways. Record signing Pallister scored the only goal on the stroke of half-time in a 1-0 win, cheekily prodding in on the line from Steve Bruce's header following a free kick by Martin. 'I think Brucie will be a bit disappointed there, as I took the goal off him,' smiled Pallister post-match. 'I just saw the ball and obviously Brucie's done great to get up and win the ball and I was just making sure, I think.'

* * *

On 14 November 1989, Manchester United lost arguably one of the most important figures in the club's history when Jimmy Murphy collapsed and died, aged 79. The club's matchday programme *United Review* paid tribute to the great man in its next edition. 'Jimmy was the man who put the fire in the bellies of the United players,' it said. 'His role with United was clearly defined from day one. He was charged with the responsibility to seek out new talent to be groomed to United's methods and standards.'

Sir Matt Busby was broken when he heard the devastating news about his right-hand man. 'It has shattered me. Jimmy and I worked together to bring greatness to United and no one outside the club will ever know how important he was to our success.' Alex Ferguson ended his next press conference with a glowing tribute to Murphy. 'I cannot close without paying tribute to Jimmy Murphy, who was still scouting for us just a few days before he died last week. He was 79 but his enthusiasm was undimmed. He used to phone me on a Sunday evening with an excitement about football which must have gripped him when he helped make Manchester United the club we know today. His love for the club was undeniable. There are certain people in life who make a lasting impression and, for me, Jimmy Murphy was such a man.'

Jimmy Murphy kept the red flag flying high and that, as Manchester United fans, is something we should be eternally grateful for. I highly recommend you read the book of the same name written by Wayne Barton, as it provides a fascinating insight into the man. God bless you, Jimmy.

***

With Ferguson's men picking up maximum points on their previous outing, the boss decided to keep the same XI as United travelled to Kenilworth Road and its famous 'plastic' pitch (more on that later) to face Luton Town. An early Danny Wallace goal after neat play by Hughes got United off to a flying start before goals from Clayton Blackmore and Hughes gave United back-to-back victories. It meant the side had won four of the previous five matches and moved up to ninth place in the table.

Wallace turned provider for United's second, sending McClair racing down the right touchline with a fantastic half-volleyed pass before the Scot sent over a delicious cross that was met on the bounce by the onrushing Blackmore, whose shot was lashed high into the net via his left boot. But the pick of the bunch was, arguably, Hughes's goal in the 76th minute. Wallace, again the source of the assist, clipped a beautiful crossfield ball into the path of Hughes, who let the ball bounce and unleashed a volley from around 25 yards that bent into the far bottom corner.

The players would have boarded the coach home after that match, counting their win bonuses before kicking back and relaxing on the journey, congratulating themselves on a job well done. But little did they know that they were about to head into a winter of discontent. For the third game in a row, Ferguson chose the same team to start the following match but, despite their best efforts, United were unable to break down a stubborn Chelsea side who were more than happy to leave Old Trafford with a point after a dull 0-0 draw.

Families across the land would have been digging around in cupboards for their Christmas decorations when United headed down to north London to face champions Arsenal at Highbury on the first weekend of December. The Gunners were looking to avenge the

4-1 hammering on the opening day of the season and show why the team from the capital had been the cream of the crop in England over the last 12 months. United rocked up in their third kit of royal blue and for the fourth match running, Ferguson sent out the same XI to take on George Graham's men.

As in the previous match, United looked tepid and uninspiring in their play, always looking to the safer option rather than trying to carve open their opponents. It was absolutely miles away from the swashbuckling performance the Old Trafford crowd were treated to back in August. Midway through the first half, a free kick played into United's box fell to the feet of winger Perry Groves and the Arsenal man lashed a shot past a diving Leighton, who could do nothing to keep out the only goal of the game in a 1-0 defeat for the Red Devils. For the second time in two matches, United had failed to threaten the scoreboard.

The manager had bemoaned bad luck with injuries following the Achilles injury new signing Webb had suffered on international duty earlier in the campaign, sidelining the midfielder for months. Webb appeared to have been a crucial cog in Ferguson's wheel and the team were missing his creative touch in the centre of the park. He seemed to have that little something different to the combative styles of both Robson and Ince. The team's play appeared to lack fluidity without Webb in the side, but the supporters were starting to see this as just another excuse following the excessive amount of money the manager had spent assembling his new-look squad.

A week later, on 9 December, came the outcry on the terraces and the straw that eventually broke the camel's back. Crystal Palace, managed by United old boy Steve Coppell, headed to Old Trafford having been taken apart by nearly every other team in the division but what unfolded, both on and off the pitch, was less than savoury. Ferguson made two changes to his side, bringing in Lee Sharpe for Mark Hughes and Russell Beardsmore for Clayton Blackmore. The latter decision appeared to have been a shrewd move when Beardsmore dived to get on the end of a Lee Martin cross after just nine minutes. But Palace battled hard to stay in the game, with goalkeeper Nigel Martyn making two smart saves from Beardsmore and McClair.

The Eagles rode their luck and got their just rewards moments before the break when a clipped ball to United's back post found a completely unmarked Mark Bright, who couldn't believe his luck as he nodded past Leighton to send the sides in at half-time level. And it was Bright, who was the scourge of United's defence all afternoon, who put the visitors into the lead just moments after the restart. Another ball into United's box was met at the front post this time by Bright, whose low, diving header seemed to squirm between Leighton and his near post and into the back of the net.

As United chased and harried, trying to get back into the match, the attention of the home supporters was drawn to events unfolding off the pitch and, most noticeably, in the stands. In an article written on *Red'n'Blue Army*, a Crystal Palace fanzine site, an away fan said of the incident: 'Not only were there chants of "Ferguson out" but a banner looking like someone's dirty old bedsheet was put up on the fencing at the Stretford End stating the same.' As we now know from the beginning of this book, the banner was the handiwork of Pete Molyneux and carried the now infamous message: '3 Years of Excuses – And It's Still Crap … Ta Ra Fergie.'

Cries of 'What a load of rubbish' and 'Fergie out' came from all corners of the stadium as the manager stood looking on at his team, who were showing no signs of snatching an equaliser. The boos rang out at full time as the manager headed down the tunnel following the 2-1 defeat. 'The reaction of our fans after our home defeat by Crystal Palace was the worst I have experienced,' admitted Ferguson the following day. The *Daily Express'* Steve Curry referenced the fact that he had 'the worst record of any United manager of modern times'. Curry warned that when the paying public become 'disenchanted, as they are doing now, then the wind of change blows in over Stretford'.

Ferguson appeared on ITV's *Sportsweek,* hosted by *The Match* presenter Elton Welsby, and looked uncomfortable over his line of questioning. 'Does it affect your confidence at all?' asked Welsby. 'Lack of success affects everyone's confidence,' replied Ferguson. 'Did you know the pressures were going to be quite as great when you left Scotland?' said Welsby, sensing an unease in the man sitting opposite him, to which Ferguson just looked directly at him before answering: 'No, I didn't realise that.' But for Ferguson, the intensity of the situation just grew.

Ferguson would later admit that the catcalls and abuse from supporters around this period started to have an impact on his private life. In the documentary *Never Give In,* he said 'I'd been at the club for just over three years and that's when the cries started. We got calls in the house, I remember that. "Go back to fucking Scotland" and all that, you know. "You're fucking useless". But I would just put the phone down. And then Cathy would get all upset.' It was a tough time for the Fergusons as a family. 'We were getting abusive phone calls,' remembered Cathy. 'I used to look out the windows at the magpies and if I only saw one, I would be looking for the other, you know. One for sorrow, two for joy.'

But there was no joy. Just seven days later, the team were again jeered off the pitch, this time following a 1-0 defeat against Tottenham Hotspur. Gary Lineker's fine curling effort heaped even more pressure on the boss, who was biting back in his interviews. Ferguson was quizzed by a reporter on his team's recent form, with the manager snapping: 'It's a hell of burden running a club that hasn't won the title for 23 years and thinks it should do every season.'

The team headed into the Christmas period with two matches on the road. First a trip to Anfield on 23 December followed by Villa Park on Boxing Day. Neither Liverpool or Aston Villa appeared likely to dish out any Christmas cheer to United. Liverpool were again flying in the league and historically as a United fan you just want to go to Anfield and not be beaten. The teams played out a 0-0 draw which, for some, would have been deemed a good result but it was yet again seen as two points dropped rather than one gained as United seemed to up their game against their biggest rivals. Ferguson's men huffed and puffed but they couldn't blow down the Anfield house and headed back to Old Trafford with just a clean sheet to show for their efforts.

Aston Villa on the other hand, were a different kettle of fish all together. United fans were left wondering if Leighton, Anderson, Bruce, Pallister, Blackmore, Martin, Ince, Phelan, Sharpe, McClair and Hughes had overdone the turkey and trimmings the day before, as it was they who were stuffed that Boxing Day when Villa ran riot in front of a full house. Kick-off was delayed by 15 minutes; such was the clamour for people to get into the ground. Mind you, this Aston Villa side were tussling at the top of the table with Arsenal and Liverpool and were in no mood to let up against a struggling United.

Bryan Robson was a noticeable absentee for the visitors, affirming what my dad had said before. No Robson, no party, was the line wheeled out on many occasions in the 1980s. To compound things for Ferguson, not only did the Villans have the young, enigmatic midfielder, David Platt, their side also contained United old boy Paul McGrath. The Republic of Ireland defender was deemed surplus to requirements by Ferguson, who shipped him out to Aston Villa, but it was McGrath who was smiling now. His partnership with Derek Mountfield at the heart of the Villa defence kept United at bay as Villa put on a show in a 3-0 win.

A chant of 'Fergie, Fergie, on the dole!' echoed around the Holte End but the cries of 'What a load of rubbish' from the travelling supporters would have been more worrying for Ferguson, a constant theme in the month of December. As Ferguson and his players traipsed towards the tunnel after the drubbing, many angry fans made their feelings known. United's display that day was pitiful, to say the least, with the manager locking the players in the dressing room for around 45 minutes after the game to let them know that the performance was completely unacceptable.

Injuries to Webb, Robson and Wallace were a real handicap to how the manager wanted to play at that time but there was still more than enough quality in the squad to ensure better performances and results. However, the team were severely lacking in confidence at a time when the manager most needed them to produce their best. 'Sparkling Villa give United a hangover,' declared the headline in *The Guardian* as the press rounded on Ferguson. 'United's board cannot continue to ignore an embarrassing run of six games without a win ... not when they've paid £13m to win the league,' wrote John Wragg in the *Daily Express*. 'Villa are a team built on strong foundations, character and ability. United are a team constructed on sand.' The knives were being sharpened as the media continued their onslaught.

Ferguson was just as brutal in his own assessment of his team. 'It was another example of the lack of consistency which has bedevilled United down the years,' he complained. 'Half a dozen of our lads don't seem to realise that you are playing Liverpool-type matches all the time with this club. After Anfield and allowing for the fact that the game obviously drained us, this was a terrible disappointment.' More pressure from the media followed, which ultimately saw the *Daily Express'* John Bean write on 28 December, under the headline 'Fergie's last stand', that a bad result in ten days' time against Nottingham Forest in the third round of the FA Cup would make his position 'untenable'.

'League games at Wimbledon on Saturday and against QPR at Old Trafford on New Year's Day are important to Ferguson's immediate future,' wrote Bean. 'But United's Cup result against Nottingham Forest is absolutely crucial ... and he knows it.' Ferguson conceded as much himself, saying: 'Everyone seems to have set the cup tie as my trial. I can cope with that because I know that I am doing the job the right way and the motivation of the players is no problem. We simply have to get on with it and remember that the game will be as hard for Forest as it will be for us.'

Worryingly, it had been three games without a goal and now, for the third game running, United were on the road, this time making a trip to Plough Lane to face Wimbledon in the last game of the decade. Young forward Mark Robins came in for Sharpe in the only change to the side and at one stage must have thought he had won the game for the visitors. Wimbledon took an early lead but Hughes prodded in at the back post on 74 minutes to bring the game level at 1-1. Just 60 seconds later, Hughes turned provider as he controlled the ball on his chest, spun his man and delivered a delicious cross that Robins headed home. That looked to be enough for all three points but Wimbledon found a last-gasp equaliser through Alan Cork as panic stations set in among the United backline and the Dons striker made them pay with a cool finish.

United saw in the New Year and a new decade by welcoming Queens Park Rangers to Old Trafford on 1 January 1990 but, with Bryan Robson still missing, the team could only muster another 0-0 draw in front of their own fans. Former United midfielder Ray Wilkins was at the heart of the QPR midfield and received a warm welcome from the Stretford End, which was probably the only cheer let out by those fans all day. Wilkins, assessing his old club's fortunes after the match, said: 'They are just lacking that little bit of confidence and that little bit of belief to just go out and play. They obviously have the talent there but it's getting that belief in themselves. They have some super players and when they string the game together, they look a terrific team.'

On 7 January, United were given some respite from the league with a trip to the City Ground in the third round of the FA Cup. The draw had seen Ferguson's men pitted against Brian Clough's Nottingham Forest, with many billing this as the game which would ultimately decide the manager's future at the club. If he was going to claim a much-needed win, he was going to have to do it again with a raft of injured players. There was speculation that captain Robson would be patched up in order to start. Ferguson, speaking on the eve of the Forest clash, said: 'If Bryan says he is fit, he will play. It goes without saying we'd rather have Bryan in the side than be without him. But that does not mean we are going to roll over and surrender if he does not play, though.' One newspaper claimed that, without Robson, United all too often looked like 'a joke'.

Leighton, Anderson, Martin, Bruce, Pallister, Phelan, Beardsmore, Blackmore, McClair, Hughes and Robins were charged with trying to keep the team in the Cup and, if the media were to be believed, keep the manager in a job. 'Every day in the lead-up to that game, we were picking up the papers and reading that the manager was facing the sack,' Viv Anderson told the *Manchester Evening News*. One red top ran the headline 'D-Day for under-fire Ferguson' and spoke of the Scot facing 'his Waterloo'. 'Things look bleak for Ferguson,' wrote respected Irish writer Eamon Dunphy. 'Clough's Forest will probably win this afternoon.' England goalkeeping legend Gordon Banks was certainly dismissive when asked to predict who would go on to win the FA Cup. 'United have no chance. They are at a low ebb,' he said.

When matchday arrived, skipper Robson was nowhere near fit enough to be in the squad and missed his fifth match in a row, which was a huge loss to the team in a period when they needed their captain the most. His troublesome groin injury would keep him out for a few more weeks yet but the show had to go on regardless of who was fit and available.

United started brightly, with Mark Robins forcing Steve Sutton in the Nottingham Forest goal into an smart save early on after a neat turn and shot as Ferguson's men looked to gain the initiative. The game became scrappy as both teams battled to break the deadlock and it was honours even as the teams hurried off at half-time. Just ten minutes after the restart and United had their noses in front. Lee Martin won possession, stretching to keep the ball in play as he began his run down the left flank before playing a short pass inside to Hughes. United's No.10 looked up and played a beautiful ball with the outside of his boot, bending the ball round the back of the forest defence for Robins to glance a header into the bottom corner.

Moments later, Hughes produced a near-carbon copy of his assist for the goal but this time the curling ball with the outside of his boot went into the arms of Sutton, who quickly sent Forest away on the counter-attack. His long kick upfield was neatly controlled by Nigel Clough, before he span and sent a pass out wide to Nigel Jemson. The Tricky Trees winger danced outside Martin and, with the goal beginning to open up to him, shot straight at the onrushing Leighton, who narrowed the angle brilliantly. With Forest now building up a head of steam, Jemson again came close when his left-footed shot flashed across the face of goal, agonisingly wide for the home supporters, who thought their team had found an equaliser.

United were hanging on but their clean sheet was still intact. Jim Leighton was screaming at his defenders to push up to try and minimise the space between defence and midfield, which was now running on empty. Then with just three minutes remaining, Forest thought that they had nabbed a late equaliser with that man Jemson again, nipping in to nod into an empty net following a free kick into the penalty area. 'Two of the matches today have already ended 1-1,' said Barry Davies on commentary for the BBC. The free kick was whipped into the box with Leighton attempting to punch clear, only for the ball to spin agonisingly into the air, but a melee of players on the floor, including Leighton, left an open goal for Jemson to equalise. And maybe this game will finish like that, too … No, the referee is going to disallow it. He's certainly being surrounded by United players. And a free kick has been given.' Just minutes later and the referee signalled the end of the match. 'At last, some respite for Alex Ferguson,' said Davies. United had only just managed to scrape through with a 1-0 win but the manager would have taken that all day long. 'I just remember a sense of relief afterwards and then also the feeling that it could be our year,' Anderson said. 'There was a renewed sense of optimism after that win. It triggered something and we turned the corner.'

The game itself was dour and lacked any real excitement, with United playing like a side who were petrified of losing. Forest could smell blood prior to kick-off but never really threatened at all in what was a pretty poor contest. Record signing Pallister helped to keep the Forest attack at bay and, according to *The Guardian's* David Lacey, ensured that the home side 'did not get a serious sight of goal until the end of the match when they pushed forward in desperate numbers'. With Des Walker playing a similarly solid role for Forest at the opposite end of the pitch, Lacey described the first half as 'tightly contested and dour to the naked eye'. It made dreary watching on television, too, but the most important thing, despite the negative reviews, was the result.

Goalscorer Robins was delighted with his contribution and his second goal in three matches. 'That is the most important goal I have scored,' commented Robins afterwards. 'It was an instinctive thing. I didn't think about trying to place it, I just headed it. It was a brilliant ball from Mark Hughes. I couldn't miss, really.' The win meant the manager had a stay of execution. 'I had no idea that goal against Nottingham Forest would become so important in the history of Manchester United,' Robins told the *Daily Telegraph* in 2016. 'How could I have known at the time?' In fact, how could anyone have known at the time? All we did know was that United were in the hat for the next round.

FA Cup Fourth Round – Less of the Bull

Venue: Edgar Street
Date: 28 January 1990
Attendance: 13,777

HAVE YOU ever been to a football match and seen a bull paraded around the ground? Well, if you had been a paying punter at Edgar Street back in the day, then this is something that would have been part of your matchday experience. It was brought to the nation's attention on 5 February 1972 when Hereford United, then of the Southern League, faced top-flight Newcastle United in the FA Cup following a 2-2 draw nearly two weeks earlier. Hereford, famous for its cattle and cider museum, was about to be overtaken by a hoard of Geordie folk.

With the weather playing havoc with football fixtures at the time, the FA decided that, after several postponements, the tie must be played on that early weekend in February, despite Hereford's pitch being deemed unplayable due to rain. Malcolm Macdonald, the Newcastle and England striker, added fuel to the fire in the build-up to the fixture when he was quoted as saying he would score ten goals in the replay at Hereford, something he later denied. 'I've taken a bit of stick because of a story that appeared before the tie that claimed I was going to beat Ted MacDougall's record of nine goals in an FA Cup game,' MacDonald recalled. 'Well, I never said that. I was a north-east football columnist and my paper saw this as an opportunity to get one over a rival. So, they made up the story saying I'd promised to score ten.'

But it wasn't just the controversial quotes about goalscoring that were dominating the build-up, the inclement weather was playing its part, too. Macdonald told *The Guardian*: 'The tie wasn't a one-day affair, it was a saga that took five postponements, two games and three weeks to complete. We were called off at St James's Park twice for rain before we finally played on 24 January, a Monday evening. The replay at Edgar Street was then called off three times. We were trying to fit in league games while seeming to live most of January in limbo land down in Worcester. The replay was scheduled for 26 January. We went down three times for it and it became a ten-day wait before we finally played the match. We packed an overnight bag for one of the trips and because we had to hang around for days, our clothes began to stink. Cecil Gees in Worcester had never known a time like it. We were their best customers. It was a very bizarre situation.'

What transpired when the fixture was finally fulfilled was something that lives on in football folklore to this very day. Macdonald thought he had won the match for the visitors with a late goal. 'Seven minutes from the end, Viv Busby knocked over a cross and I headed in. We thought it was finally over,' remembered 'Supermac'. But what was to unfold in a crazy chain of events prompted the BBC to make the match its main game on *Match of the Day* that night, trumping even a fourth-round clash between First Division heavyweights Liverpool and Leeds United.

With just minutes remaining, a midfielder by the name of Ronnie Radford catapulted himself into the living rooms of millions and the memories of so many more. When Radford played a neat one-two with Brian Owen, the return pass bobbled up on a pitch that was now resembling a cow field. Fitting indeed for a club nicknamed the Bulls. Although the ball bounced awkwardly on the muddy surface, it sat up kindly for Radford to unleash a strike from around 30 yards that, in the words of commentator John Motson, 'flew into the top corner of McFaul's net'. Motson was excitable in his commentary but who could blame him after that hit? 'What a goal! What a goal! Radford the scorer … Ronnie Radford,' he proclaimed to the viewers at home. What followed were scenes of ecstasy in the stands and a pitch invasion by hundreds of fans, pictures that would be replayed on TV for decades to come.

The game went into extra time and substitute Ricky George won the match for the hosts when his turn and shot evaded the grasp of McFaul in the Newcastle goal to spark the second pitch invasion of the afternoon. Hereford's 2-1 win was the biggest FA Cup upset ever recorded in the competition. 'We hit the bar, we hit the post, the keeper made tremendous saves,' said Macdonald. 'You would think Ricky would never have a bit of luck like that again but, of course, he did. He bought a jumper that won the Grand National in 1998 called Earth Summit.'

Everyone loves a giant-killing in the Cup, especially when it comes from a team much lower down in the rankings. There have been other fabulous examples of this over the years, such as Colchester United upsetting Leeds United in 1971, Bournemouth picking the pockets of holders Manchester United in 1984, Sutton United 2 Coventry City 1 in 1988 and Wrexham beating Arsenal in 1991. It is these occasions that, in my opinion, make the FA Cup the greatest knockout cup competition in the world.

To put these giant-killings into context, Colchester, like Hereford a year later, were a Fourth Division outfit, pitting their wits against the mighty Leeds United under Don Revie. And did you hear the one about Manchester United travelling to Dean Court as FA Cup holders to take on Harry Redknapp's Cherries, only to be sent packing back to M16 with a 2-0 defeat by the Third Division side? Sutton United were a non-league club when they dispatched First Division Coventry, who had won the FA Cup two seasons earlier, and probably didn't care less when they went on to lose 8-0 in the next round against Norwich City. And finally, we have Welsh outfit Wrexham. Despite being a few divisions below the First Division champions, Arsenal, they knocked out the Gunners 2-1, with Mickey Thomas scoring an absolutely majestic free kick.

It's these games that become cemented in the memory and ones we look back on fondly as the years pass, with each season offering the possibility of a big team having their scalp taken. Fans travel the length and breadth of the country to watch every minute of their heroes, hoping that their team can be the one to slay the dragons of the top division. For Hereford and their fans, another chance to seize the day presented itself when the draw for the FA Cup fourth round was made and the Bulls were handed a plum home tie against Alex Ferguson's Manchester United.

Hereford fan David Griffin grew up in a family of Manchester United fans but in 1980, his parents swapped the city life for a taste of the countryside and moved from Manchester down to Hereford. 'I'm from the reddest of families,' said Griffin. 'Dad was born in Manchester in 1938. He saw the Busby Babes week in week out and was even at Wembley in 1968 to see us win the big one. My two brothers and I were indoctrinated from birth and it's the glue that has bound us ever since. No matter what problems of growing up, or being grown up, that we had, we could always talk United.'

Having relocated, Griffin still used to split his time between adoring his first love United and his new sweetheart of the other United, Hereford. 'I was born in 1973 and started going to Hereford with mates from school in around 1988. At the same time, a mate and I would get the supporters' bus up to United whenever we could. I was 15. It's astonishing Mum even let me go! We used to stand in the Paddock at Old Trafford because we thought it was rowdier than the Stretford End. I was tiny back then and could only usually see about 20 per cent of the action if I was lucky.'

To reach the fourth round of the FA Cup, Hereford had started their run from round one and had already seen off Farnborough Town 1-0, Merthyr Tydfil 3-2 and Walsall 2-1, the latter a barnstorming match that saw the Bulls come from a goal down with just minutes remaining, turning the tie on its head to win late on. Goals from Mark Jones and Mel Pejic sealed the win to enable a shot at writing another footballing legend. Jones had signed from Walsall just months earlier, so it was bittersweet for the midfielder, who slotted away his penalty to bring the game back to 1-1. 'I was still living in Walsall at the time. Lots of my friends were in the away end. I had a lot of banter off them during the week but I put that at the back of my mind and got on with the job,' said Jones.

David Griffin recalls the scenes when Hereford scored the winner. 'I can remember that third-round weekend. We played Walsall at home, 1-0 down with five minutes to go, a penalty, then our centre midfielder Pejic, who hadn't left the centre circle for years, bursting through to score. In front of us on the Meadow End! A few of my mates went over the wall and on to the pitch. I used to say I had but I think I was too scared or just too short to get over the wall. Then the fourth-round draw, Hereford against United at home. The town went insane.' So much so that the local radio station put out a seven-inch single called 'Up for the Cup', which featured the immortal chorus: 'Up for the cup, up for the cup, Radio Wyvern and Hereford are up for the cup.'

Fresh from United's heroics at the City Ground, the team were at home the following week for the second consecutive league match, with Derby County making the trip up Warwick Way to face Ferguson's men, who were riding the crest of a wave following their third-round victory in the FA Cup. The boss kept an unchanged side as he looked to try and build on the momentum from the week previous, and with the club sitting in 15th position, there was a real feeling that the worm had turned. All it needed now was a couple of good performances followed by some positive results and the mood around the place would be lifted.

But the adrenalin from the Forest game soon wore off and with just ten minutes on the clock, Steve Bruce was sent for an early bath following a rash challenge on Derby striker Dean Saunders. The Welsh international had skipped away from Bruce, who could only lunge at the forward, giving the referee an early decision to make and his conclusion was that he had to show United's No.4 a red card. When you are scrambling for form in football, the decisions usually go against you, with your team not getting the rub of the green. Bruce's red card was a tough pill to swallow but it was one Ferguson's men had to swallow, nonetheless.

Then, on the stroke of half-time, Derby took the lead with a goal that possibly Bruce himself may have helped prevent. A corner from the left was swung out towards the far post and there was Mark Wright to loop his header over a body of players and land just inside the opposite post. United were only marking one post and not the one his header went in at, so was this due to the reduction of players and a gamble that did not pay off? Just minutes after the restart and the men in red restored parity when Clayton Blackmore's chipped free kick was nodded down by Viv Anderson into the path of Gary Pallister, who prodded the ball past England goalkeeper Peter Shilton from seven yards out.

The Rams kept knocking on the door though, and eventually, with the ten men beginning to wilt, it opened. A cross from the left managed to find its way to

Nick Pickering, who swung his boot and guided the ball into Jim Leighton's far corner. By now, United were dead on their feet and, despite goalscorer Wright receiving his second yellow card of the day and making his way to join Bruce in the players' lounge slightly earlier than anticipated, it was too little, too late for Ferguson's men, who were now just blowing.

The defeat left United stuck in 15th place and another defeat cast doubt over whether the FA Cup victory over Nottingham Forest was just a flash in the pan. The beauty of the FA Cup is that you generally only have to be good on the day, except, of course, if the match goes to a replay. The draw for the fourth round of the competition had been kind to Ferguson and his men, pitting them against Fourth Division opposition but before they headed south towards the west country, there was the small matter of a televised game at Carrow Road, where an out-of-form Norwich City lay in wait.

Ferguson had Danny Wallace returning from injury and his return was the only change to the side, with Clayton Blackmore dropping to the bench. With Wallace back in the side, Ferguson would have been hoping that a little extra pace in the wide areas would get United further up the pitch. The Canaries had lost their last four in a row but that was peanuts compared to United's run of ten matches without their players receiving a win bonus. On ITV's *Big Match*, United huffed and puffed again but Norwich looked the more comfortable over the course of the afternoon and when Robert Fleck struck twice in the last 15 minutes, the writing was on the wall for another dismal defeat.

It was another performance that lacked any real fight, even with the tenacious tackling of Paul Ince, who missed his partner in crime, Robson. His absence from the team was, as always, particularly noticeable. The defeat meant the club dropped two places down the table into 17th, hovering precariously over the trapdoor to the Second Division. Surely United couldn't go down? Their squad was far too good to be relegated but this, of course, had happened before. Ferguson kept a brave face in front of the media and voiced his displeasure at the performance but the manager had a joker up his sleeve, with the team still fighting in the FA Cup.

Never mind jokers, it was tickets that people were now clamouring for in Hereford. With the Red Devils coming to play, an admission stub was the hottest ticket in town. 'Everybody in the city wanted to go,' said Griffin. 'They put up a temporary stand, I think. There was a voucher system in place, so you had to go to at least one, maybe two or three home games to get a voucher to let you buy a cup ticket. I remember people paying through the turnstile and immediately walking back out, voucher in hand. My dad knew the team doctor. I think he got a pair through him. He was sitting in the stand on the dugout side with my brother, Jonah. I was on the Meadow End.'

Cup fever gripped Hereford, with local legend Danny Lee singing 'Hereford United, We All Love You', a song he had written himself, and out came the famous Hereford bull to be paraded prior to kick-off. United headed to Edgar Street on 28 January 1990 with a squad peppered with internationals and they lined up with Leighton, Anderson, Martin, Donaghy, Duxbury, Pallister, Blackmore, Ince, McClair, Hughes and Wallace. Captain Robson was still missing through injury but, apart from that, it was a very strong side the manager was able to choose. He had to go as close to full strength as he could. This was possibly the last roll of the dice for Ferguson as he looked to navigate his way into the fifth round.

United started the match with a cagey look about them, looking to try and contain the hosts before imposing themselves on the game, but it was Hereford who looked like opening the scoring when a ball from Tester on the left flank found its way into the middle of United's penalty area, only for Jon Narbett's effort to fall narrowly past Leighton's upright. The Bulls midfielder's eyes must have lit up as he met the ball but it was agonisingly wide. This seemed to spark the Red Devils into life and it was the man nicknamed 'Sparky' who went closest for the visitors.

Hughes picked up the ball on the halfway line, down on the nearside touchline, and skipped past his marker with ease. The Welshman continued his run down the wing before playing a slide rule ball into the path of McClair. With a defender for company, he simply moved one way then the other before slipping the ball back to his mate Hughes. United's No.10 took a touch that seemed to bobble away from him on the mudbath of a pitch but, leaning back and stretching out his left boot, he managed to get a shot away that curled just the wrong way past the far post.

An interesting fact from that day provided by David Griffin was that the Hereford United fanzine *Talking Bull* labelled Mark Hughes as a 'one-man commando unit'. I mean, they weren't wrong, were they? And it was Hughes again moments later who should have broken the deadlock when his half-volley from ten yards was well saved by Hereford stopper Elliot. Neither team looked like they could find a way through but Hereford should have capitalised when a whistle blown from the crowd caused United's defence to stop, thinking the referee had blown his whistle. It was a bizarre incident and, fortunately, one that didn't have any severe consequences.

Hereford huffed and puffed in the second half, trying to dampen the fires as wave after wave of United attacks poured down on their goal. The home fans must have sensed that a money-spinning trip to Old Trafford was in the offing as they began to sing 'You'll Never Walk Alone', which was met with boos from the away fans. But with just six minutes remaining, United finally found a way through the stern rearguard of Peacock and Hemming. Darren Peacock would move on from Hereford and have a successful career at Queens Park Rangers and then Newcastle United during their glory years under Kevin Keegan. On this day, against United, he and his defensive partner were imperious.

Even with the pitch now resembling a pile of mashed potato with gravy all over it, United still managed to string together a few passes before Mike Duxbury made a lung-busting run into the box, evaded the men in muddy white shirts and squared the ball across the six-yard box for an unmarked Clayton Blackmore to fire home. He couldn't miss. Now it was the United fans who were in full voice as Hereford's players and supporters looked shellshocked and sapped of all energy. The referee blew his whistle to signal the end of the contest and, by the skin of their teeth, United were victorious at Edgar Street.

David Griffin would have been one of those fans who were just moments away from savouring more history. 'Before the start, we paraded a bull, a big-game staple, always humiliating for us fans,' said Griffin. 'I think the Meadow End sang 'You'll Never Walk Alone' and held scarves in a Liverpool style before the start. I was disgusted. The game was awful. I think we (Hereford, I was very confused and conflicted) had an opportunity but someone in the crowd blew a whistle and our lad stopped. Then United scored a tap-in from a cross, right in front of us, late on. Huge chants of 'We're proud of you' from us echoed the stadium. I met Dad in the car park afterwards. He was very happy, buzzing for the win that took United to the next round. I was numb. Obviously, I was a United fan and I should have been happy but I was so upset for Hereford. I think I wanted a replay, a trip to Old Trafford and we could lose there.'

The game itself was nothing to write home about but it will forever be remembered for 13,777 fans cramming into Edgar Street and the Bulls being just six minutes away from earning a lucrative replay. Another who reminisces about that day is third-round hero Mark Jones, who said he will always remember the atmosphere and how the game was nearly called off due to the heavy rain that caused the Merton Meadow car park to be flooded for the first time. 'We expected the game to be called off because, when we got to the ground, there was mud everywhere. We had three days in Torquay because it took us completely away from playing football and the whole city was buzzing about playing Man United,' said Jones, who is now a 47-year-old lorry driver living near Walsall.

'Clayton Blackmore won it for them six minutes from time, which was gutting. I lost the ball in my own half and they went on to score, which was a bit gutting personally and for the club. The thing they always bang on about is the Nottingham Forest game and how Alex Ferguson would have been out of a job if Man United had lost. But I'm pretty sure if we had beaten them, he would have been out.' But Alex Ferguson lived to fight another day, again by the narrowest of margins. Someone was clearly looking down on him. They say that if you can't play well, make sure you're still in the draw for the next round. United did exactly that ... just.

As a side note, Ronnie Radford's wonderful effort against Newcastle United in 1972 won goal of the season on the BBC and his celebration was featured in the opening title sequence of *Match of the Day* for years. After Radford's football career finished, he went back to being a carpenter but was given the prestigious honour of presenting the annual 'Giant-Killing Award' that was presented at half-time during the FA Cup Final each season. Sadly, Radford passed away in November 2022.

FA Cup Fifth Round – Tyne to Work

Venue: St James' Park

Date: 18 February 1990

Attendance: 31,748

OLDFIELD, MORLEY, Bishop, Oldfield and Hinchcliffe. You can be forgiven if you think I might be going mad but those players' names will forever be etched in my memory of the day that Manchester City stuck five past a hapless United back in the September 1989. 'It was the most embarrassing defeat of my career,' said Ferguson and, when quizzed about his team's defence, he quipped: 'It was like climbing a glass mountain. I've never seen a worse defensive display in all my career.' In more recent times, there have been a couple of drubbings from those across the way but back then it had been years since one of the sides really put the other to the sword in the way of a victory by a large margin.

The first official league fixture between the sides, way back on 3 November 1894, was one of the highest-scoring games ever between the city rivals as United ran out victorious, winning 5-2 away at City (who then played at Hyde Road). There were almost as many goals scored in a match between them even earlier than that in their first FA Cup meeting over three years earlier on 3 October 1891, when United once again prevailed, this time 5-1 at home (then North Road). There had been a sprinkling of occasions, however, when one or other of the sides has won by a five-goal margin (though never any more than that). It's interesting to note that all the biggest wins before that dark day in September came at Old Trafford and, perhaps rather surprisingly, they all went the way of City. There was a 6-1 win for City in January 1926, a 5-0 hammering in February 1955 and a 4-1 beating (courtesy of a Francis Lee hat-trick) in December 1970.

Manchester United's next fixture in the 1989/90 season was the Manchester derby at Old Trafford. All eyes were back on the league calendar as the Red Devils looked to avenge the heavy defeat at Maine Road a few months earlier. Manchester City midfielder Paul Lake was relishing the opportunity of doing the double over their city rivals. 'Our only successes had really been winning the FA Youth Cup, getting promoted from the Second Division and then holding our own in the First Division. If you had a bit of a cup run, that was an okay season. Other than that, the main event was the Manchester derby, which was hugely significant for our season.' Lake had been instrumental in the 5-1 mauling, so would have been licking his lips at the prospect of taking on Ferguson's men, who were still winless in the league since early November.

Leighton, Anderson, Pallister, Donaghy, Martin, Duxbury, Phelan, Blackmore, Wallace, McClair and Hughes ran out of the Old Trafford tunnel determined to set the record straight. And they looked to have grabbed all three points when the previous week's hero at Hereford, Clayton Blackmore, swooped down low to nod in a fine cross from Danny Wallace to send the Stretford End into raptures with just under 20 minutes remaining. Unfortunately, just three minutes later, City found a way back into the match through an Ian Brightwell strike and that meant Ferguson's men had now gone 11 league matches without a win – their worst run since the 1971/72 season. The moans and groans from the fans were still audible around the ground as the supporters filtered out on to the streets around the Trafford Park industrial estate, with plenty to chew on when heading back home via the local ale houses.

With the team now sitting in 17th, hazardously close to the relegation trapdoor, the bookmakers slashed the odds on United being relegated to just 5/2. I mean, it wasn't beyond the realms of possibility. It had happened a handful of times before, with the team tumbling into the Second Division as recently as the 1973/74 campaign, just a few years after the ecstasy of winning the European Cup. Wayne Barton has written the book *Too Good to Go Down* in which he expertly documents the team around that time and all their trials and tribulations, something similar to how this team was being perceived. With wins for Ferguson seemingly hard to come by, the team lurched closer and closer to relegation becoming a reality.

United's next fixture was a tricky trip to south London to face Millwall at The Den. The Lions had also been enduring a sticky patch results-wise and were winless in six matches, with the natives getting restless on the terraces. Ferguson's men had thumped their hosts 5-1 back in September, so United fans could have been forgiven for thinking that this could be the game which would break the team's recent duck. Russell Beardsmore replaced Mal Donaghy in the only change to the side after the Manchester derby, with the red-hot Clayton Blackmore again starting in midfield.

It was the home side who began the brighter of the two and in the 26th minute, a superb looping header from Darren Morgan sent the Cold Blow Lane End wild. United were unable to clear their lines and were eventually punished for their rotten defending when a cross from the left found Morgan near the penalty spot and, despite the best efforts of two men in red, he glanced his header past Leighton and into the far-left hand corner. United rallied after the break and when a fine piece of wing play by Beardsmore was headed back across goal by Hughes, Danny Wallace was on hand to fire home from close range, via a nick off the inside of the post. Beardsmore had given his full-back twisted blood as he bamboozled the Lions defender before digging out a sublime back-post delivery.

Hughes the provider then turned match-winner. Gary Pallister drove out of the defence towards the halfway line before playing a neat pass into the feet of goalscorer Wallace. The forward set the ball back to McClair and he, in turn, played a neat pass out to the left for substitute Robins to run on to. Turning back inside his marker, Robins laid the ball back to Lee Martin and he drove inside from the left flank before playing a beautiful slide rule reverse pass between centre-back and right-back into the path of Wallace. He squared the ball across the six-yard box where Hughes, arriving on the spot at the right moment, swept home to spark a huge roar from the travelling support. It was a fantastic passage of play that resulted in the winning goal.

This 2-1 win in the league had been well overdue. Those three points on the road at The Den lifted Ferguson's side to 15th and gave them a little breathing space, especially with a break from First Division duty as league action gave way to another weekend in the FA Cup, with United drawn against another United in the shape of Second Division Newcastle. Ferguson later described December 1989 as 'the darkest period he had ever suffered in the game' and he was hoping the win against Millwall in February would turn the tide on United's fortunes.

Newcastle had been relegated from the First Division the previous season and were bidding to bounce back at the first attempt. A 5-2 opening day walloping of fellow title contenders Leeds United gave the Geordie faithful renewed hope that this campaign was going to be a success, despite there being some unrest amongst the fans over the way the club was being run. New signings Micky Quinn and Mark McGhee, a key man for Ferguson at Aberdeen, had formed a formidable partnership at the spearhead of the Magpies' attack but Quinn must have wondered what he had walked into when he arrived at the club to hear chants of 'sack the board' and read a banner that asked 'Who the fuck is Mick Quinn?'

Quinn had scored four goals on his debut in that demolition job on Leeds and was licking his lips at the thought of creating an upset in the cup. The striker had managed to win over the fans in his first match and, recalling how he celebrated his hat-trick goal that day, said: 'I went nuts and ran towards the Gallowgate, arms outstretched. "That's who fucking Mick Quinn is!" I screamed, almost tearful.' The goals kept on coming that season and the Magpies were imperious at home, scoring fives against Leeds United and Leicester City and only once failing to score in front of their own supporters.

Newcastle had been handed a tricky third round tie away to Hull City but secured a narrow 1-0 win courtesy of a Liam O'Brien goal in the 67th minute. After some neat build-up play from the Magpies, a piece of brilliance from Quinn set up the onrushing O'Brien to fire home from the edge of the penalty area. The fourth-round draw saw the Magpies on the road again, this time heading to Reading to play out a rip-roaring 3-3 draw. Both teams would have to do it all again back at St James' Park but this time the boys in black and white stripes made no mistake in a 4-1 hammering of the Royals. Mark McGhee notched a brace alongside a goal apiece from Quinn and David Robinson. The team from the Tyne were certainly in good nick heading into this cup tie.

'Context is everything when viewing events through life's rearview mirror,' said United fan Pete Molyneux. 'Fixtures between these two northern Uniteds graced many decades since the dawn of professional football in England but, at the start of the 90s, the gloss had faded. Newcastle were battling for promotion from the second tier whilst the Red Devils fought a desperate relegation battle to stay in the First Division through that winter. But an FA Cup run can bring welcome relief and hope for fans, players and managers alike.'

'Molly' had travelled to St James' Park despite the feelings of discontent earlier in the winter that had prompted him to unfurl his banner back in December, calling for the manager's head. 'It was certainly with hope that we travelled early that Sunday morning, 18 February,' he said. 'We actually travelled in my mate

Tezzer's new company car, a plush little number. Cars had become our choice of awayday travel by the late 80s. Football fans had a bit more disposable income by then, so long gone were the days of a sedate 52-seater coach, the 'Hooligan Express' run by British Rail or reckless ventures with 15 Reds crammed into a Salford Van Hire transit.' He and his friends were the epitome of what it meant to follow Manchester United across the land during those times.

'The third match of this year's cup run was the third consecutive away tie, each one played on a Sunday afternoon as live TV matches became the norm in the UK,' said Molly. 'No sleepy lay-in then for me, Tez, Bri or Steve. We'd followed United home and way since the 60s and already seen some great years where United became the first English side to lift the European Cup, win two league titles, plus three FA Cups in the 70s and 80s. But we'd won nothing for five years and, for Manchester United, that's a long time. Seems crazy to say it but we had little (if any) faith in current manager, Alex Ferguson, changing things soon. United sat 16th out of 20 teams in the league, just two places above the relegation places. A week before the Newcastle cup game, we'd won 2-1 at Millwall – our first league victory since 18 November 1989; a total of 11 games without a victory. "Hard winter" doesn't start to describe it.'

The journey up was filled with discussions on the previous two matches, as well as the prospect of a potential banana skin awaiting. 'After a general catch-up on the first part of the journey, conversation amongst us turned to our chances of reaching the next round,' remembers Molyneux. 'The 1-0 wins at Forest and Hereford had lifted spirits but this Man United side were playing very disjointed football. Games were often scrappy. Newcastle had a great FA Cup history but most of those deeds were now consigned to history lessons.'

For all the positive pieces of FA Cup history the Magpies had created, who could forget the events detailed in the previous chapter when a certain Ronnie Radford sent Newcastle packing back to the Tyne with their tails between their legs?

Back in 1990, there was still the element of football violence, an added jeopardy when travelling to away matches and one 'Molly' and his pals were well versed in trying to avoid. 'As we got closer to Newcastle, talk inevitably turned to what reception United fans might expect from the Geordies and what plans we'd put in place to park the car in a safe place and not far from the stadium,' said Molyneux. 'I'd been chased round Newcastle town centre a few times in the 70s. It was a rough city and they still sought revenge for the mid-late 1960s when the Stretford End regularly took the Leazes, their home end. St James' Park was undergoing a refurb and the ground would hold just under 32,000 compared to high 50 thousands in days gone by. We parked near the United coaches and latched on to the police escort to the ground. We were lucky. No attacks came our way. Perhaps it was a Sunday thing?'

Leighton, Anderson, Martin, Bruce, Phelan, Pallister, Robins, Duxbury, McClair, Hughes and Wallace were Ferguson's selected XI as the team looked to build a winning streak. The last time back-to-back wins were achieved was back in early November but all of a sudden there seemed to be a little spring in the step of both the manager and the players. Newcastle, however, had taken four points off Ferguson's United the previous campaign, so they were hardly going to be too concerned about what was going to be served up in front of them on their own turf. It was going to be a different challenge for United to the one at Hereford but a tough task, nonetheless.

'Molly' was kind enough to give me his memories of the match that day, as well as his recollection of the journey and rounds previous. His words seem to capture the tone perfectly as United looked to overturn a tricky opponent. 'The pitch was well worn of grass, as was the case by February in those days, and the wind blew strong,' said Molyneux. 'Conditions made for a match that was anything but free-flowing. If my account sems a little downbeat, please be reassured I'm not "Pessimistic Pete". I'm very much a cup half-full supporter. But I've tried to convey the general mood around the club and this particular match.

'So, let's get to the good part. The one vital ingredient the game had was goals. Even more vital, more goals went in their net than ours! United's line-up was a familiar one. Since the autumn, we'd been robbed of Bryan Robson and Neil Webb due to long-term injuries. Both England internationals, their absence had bitten hard in terms of quality in midfield. Loyal foot soldiers Mike Duxbury, Clayton Blackmore and Mike Phelan had manfully covered their roles but lacked the magic dust that transforms good sides to great. Promising youngster Lee Sharpe and veteran Viv Anderson also missed much of the winter through injuries. The situation wasn't unsimilar to Ten Hag's challenges in 23/24.

'Before Christmas 1989, strikers Hughes and McClair struggled to deliver the goals and 20-year-old reserve-team striker Mark Robins was given his chance and grabbed it with both hands. I felt United started well. Our attacks featured good passing play, though the end result was a little blunt. Players in red seemed more fleet of foot away from the weekly relegation battles. Around 19 minutes in, tricky winger Danny Wallace won and took a corner right in front of United's away following. His cross sailed over the six-yard box, missing most players, but found Robins, who glanced a header just inside the far post. United held the lead and went in 1-0 up at the break.

'We could have doubled that lead shortly after the break but Burridge saved. On 50 minutes, the usually composed Steve Bruce tripped Mark McGee in the box. The Geordie striker thumped the spot kick past Leighton and raised the tempo on the home terraces. The noise would have unsettled most visiting teams but ten minutes later, Wallace took a ball in his stride as he raced into the area, then slotted home from a really tight angle. Five minutes later, Kevin Scott headed Newcastle level from a corner after United keeper Leighton was barged to the ground. The goal stood; it was the proverbial seesaw match. A real cut-and-thrust cup tie had broken out and it could have gone either way.

'United were forced back and had to defend deep. On the terraces, we'd have taken a replay at that point. But United broke quickly on 72 minutes, Ince hit a long ball down to Wallace, who raced through then squared it to McClair to slot home and send the away end into raptures. The Scottish striker had gone 17 games without a goal and his joy was unbounded. The goal settled United and, though Newcastle threw everything at us, we kept our shape, dug in and saw the match out for a 3-2 win. The joy on the United terraces was raucous and sustained. God knows, we'd had little to celebrate since the clocks had gone back the previous October. But the sixth round beckoned. We knew our opponents before we left St James', another tier two club, Sheffield United. It would be away but it felt there may just be a wind of change in United's performances and results. Two more victories would take us to a Wembley final. Dare we dream yet?'

Jim Smith in the Newcastle dugout was close but no cigar to forcing a replay that could have potentially caused an upset. 'Yeah, that's the thing when you go in against Fergie. You almost do the job and his team keep coming back,' remembered Smith. 'But we rattled them that day. You could say we almost changed history, eh? They had to earn a win. We lost narrowly and focused our attentions back on the league.' With time ticking away towards the end of the game, when both Smith and Ferguson were prowling in front of their dugouts, the BBC cameras captured a lovely moment which demonstrated the desperation of both bosses, who hugged each other as the final few seconds passed. One was seeing the chance of a giant-killing slip through his fingers like quicksilver while the other had the look of a man extending his role of employment just a little longer.

The fires in the engine of the Manchester United locomotive were beginning to burn white hot in the FA Cup as the team hurtled down the track towards the quarter-finals. A tricky trip to Bramall Lane awaited the men from Old Trafford but the win at Newcastle gave the manager much needed breathing space, a commodity that was as priceless as the victory that day itself. Back on the bus, the team headed south back to M16 with thoughts of better days filling the staff and players' minds. Even the rain had stopped. Maybe there really was something in the air that day.

FA Cup Sixth Round – Bassett's Blades, Blunted

Venue: Bramall Lane
Date: 11 March 1990
Attendance: 34,344

'I WAS always up for a laugh – work hard, play hard.' That was the mantra of Sheffield United boss Dave 'Harry' Bassett. It was something that rubbed off on his players wherever he managed, starting his career in the dugout at Wimbledon, where he became a household name, before a brief stint at Watford that didn't quite work out. Not to be deterred, Bassett had departed Vicarage Road with his head held high and was again on the move. This time he ventured out of London, heading north to the 'Steel City' of Sheffield where he would find a squad and a club that were in decline. On his arrival, Bassett was thrust straight in front of the media. In his first press conference, he said: 'I could have done with a rest from the game but when a club as big as United comes along, you have to wonder if it will still be on the market when you are ready to start again. You can be out of football too long and quickly become forgotten. There is a love of the game up here that is perhaps missing in London and the south. Frankly, if there had been a job going in London right now, I would not have taken it.'

With the Blades languishing near the bottom of the Second Division in January 1988, Bassett joined in the hope of turning around the club's fortunes. Despite his best efforts, though, the club tumbled into the third tier of English football. Even though Bassett had only been with the club for the second half of the campaign, the manager shouldered some of the responsibility and was disappointed not to have helped project the club in an upward trajectory. He found that wins were hard to come by, as the team looked completely shot of any confidence. The run those players were on before his arrival had completely broken their resilience and the team continued to play out poor performances, culminating in the eventual relegation. 'Harry' knew he had a job on his hands and his assessment of the playing staff was short and to the point. 'On that evidence, the team is not good enough,' he said. 'There is a battle ahead and I need players who will battle. They did not have enough fire in their bellies.'

Bassett's story is quite incredible and one that hardly attracts the credit it thoroughly deserves in any debate about great managers. The Londoner captained

Wimbledon back in the old Southern League days during the 1970s, a time when the club finally earned election to the Football League. On his retirement, he joined the management team at the club under the stewardship of Dario Gradi. Then, in 1981, Bassett was given the chance to take charge of the side when Gradi departed Plough Lane to take the manager's job at Crystal Palace.

The Dons would embark on a 12-game winning run from the moment Bassett took the job that January, before a slight blip threatened to undo the good work he had started. The team managed to shake off the slight run of bad form and put together another string of good results, culminating in Wimbledon nicking a promotion spot. The Dons had reached the Third Division, the highest placing in the club's history. 'Off Dario went to Selhurst Park and it was down to me and then came that 12-match unbeaten run,' said Bassett. 'The players were brilliant, especially given all the off-field shenanigans. They just got on with their jobs, gave their all and churned out results.' And there really were some goings-on behind the scenes in regard to players and staff getting involved in what we would today call 'banter'.

Wimbledon quickly gained the reputation of being a team with an excellent workrate and an even better team spirit. Bassett was at the centre of all that was good at the club and he did it on a shoestring budget, something that you would find very difficult to achieve in the game nowadays. In his six seasons in charge, Bassett masterminded two promotions from the Fourth Division, with a relegation sandwiched in between. Consecutive promotions followed, as the club leapt from the Fourth Division to the second tier in just three seasons. By 1986, they had reached the top flight of English football.

It's a remarkable achievement considering the financial restraints the club operated under. Heralding from a small corner of south-west London, they were battling against the likes of Chelsea, Fulham, Queens Park Rangers and, even further afield, Arsenal, Tottenham Hotspur and West Ham United. The club grew at a rate that was unforeseen, so they had to cut their cloth accordingly at all times. In the book *Crazy Gang*, Bassett said: 'We had terrific spirit but no money. Because a team bus cost too much, chairman Ron Noades ordered players to drive to Rochdale, just like a pub side. Mind you, even when we did have a bus, like on that trip to Swansea, we left Dave Galvin behind at the service station and he missed the match!'

When Harry walked out of the club in the summer of 1987 following a dispute over his contract, he left behind a team that would go on to lift the FA Cup the following season. Wimbledon 1 Liverpool 0 shook the football world, with the Merseysiders hoping to complete a league and cup double until commentator

John Motson delivered the immortal line 'The Crazy Gang have beaten the Culture Club', as the referee signalled the end of the contest. In just ten years, the club had hurtled from the depths of non-league football to being an established top-flight club who then went on to win the FA Cup. Bobby Gould guided the Dons to glory that season but it was a foundation built on Bassett's team.

The togetherness of the players and management made the team tick, as well as Bassett's eye for a bargain signing. 'I look for talent, whether he's got something about him,' said Bassett. 'It's a gut feeling. Then I ask myself "Does he understand the game? Is he athletic? Is he brave? Is his character sound?"' Couple that with the man-management and team bonding Bassett created and you have a winning recipe. The team were known as the 'Crazy Gang' and for good reason. With money tight and facilities less than adequate, the manager knew he had to find other ways of enhancing performances.

'With the Crazy Gang, the players were young and I encouraged them,' said Bassett. 'We enjoyed the banter. I used to make the lads do what we called the A3 run through Richmond, up to Wimbledon Village and back. I joined them one time and, as I came back into the training area, they grabbed me, slung me in a puddle and roared off! I turned a blind eye to a few things.' But 'Harry' put his trust in all his players. 'I'd say "I'll treat you like adults, so behave like adults". If we were

Alex Ferguson reports for duty having just taken the job at Old Trafford.

The manager splashed the cash on new signings in the summer of 1989 with Neil Webb primed to be the midfield playmaker.

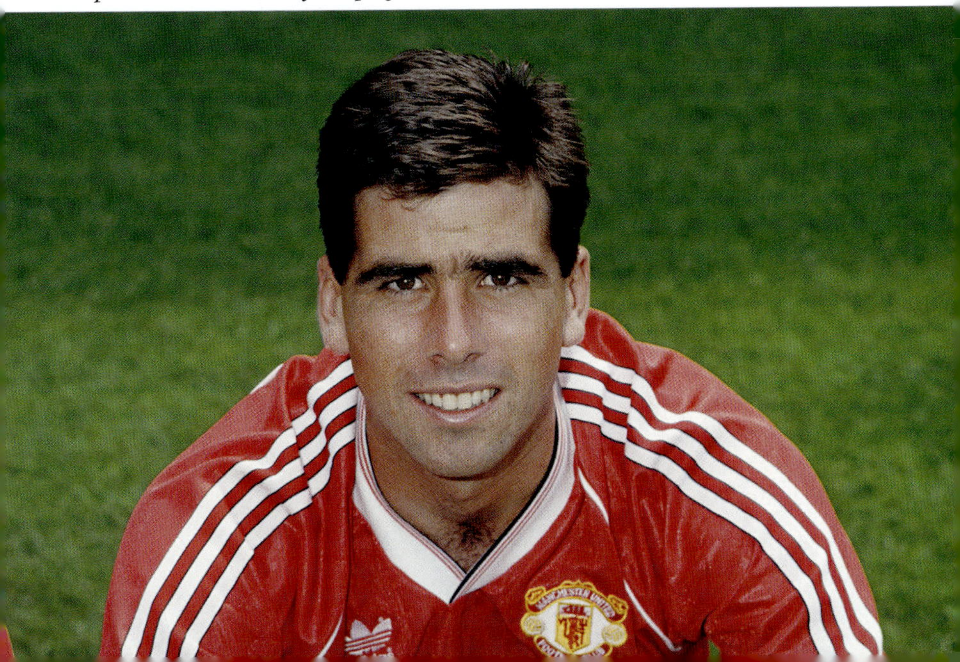

Michael Knighton had agreed a deal in principal with Martin Edwards to buy the club. The news broke just days before the start of the 1989/90 season.

Knighton was introduced to the Old Trafford faithful by producing a few ball tricks, before firing into the goal at the Stretford End.

Steve Bruce opened the scoring in a 4-1 win over Champions Arsenal but a title charge was ended as the clocks changed in October.

City score again on that black day that we would rather not talk about.

Mark Robins celebrates the only goal in a 1-0 win over Nottingham Forest to kick-start the cup run.

Jim Leighton in animated mood following the 3-2 win against Newcastle United.

Robins is carried off by fans after scoring the winner in the semi-final replay. United were heading to Wembley.

Hallworth and Leighton embrace following two matches that produced 9 goals over two matches.

Leighton and Bruce fail to clear Gary O'Reilly's header that gave Crystal Palace the lead.

Big game player Mark Hughes equalises to make the scoreline 3-3 and ensure there would be a replay.

Goal scorer Lee Martin is bundled to the floor after scoring the winner. The goal was arguably the most important in United's history.

On loan goalkeeper Les Sealey kept a clean sheet after his shock inclusion had sparked a huge debate prior to kick-off.

Martin proudly holds the FA Cup above his head. Little did he know that
his goal provided the catalyst of the modern day United.

rubbish on the Saturday, I wouldn't bother to discuss it then. I'd say "See you tomorrow, ten o'clock sharp", and they knew they'd be in Sunday morning.'

The manager was a shrewd operator and the players knew what was expected of them. And if they didn't, then they were certainly reminded of it. Daniel Taylor, writing for *The Guardian* in 2015, stated: 'It might not fit into the stereotype of this homespun club, where the players stole traffic cones for what passed as a training ground and there was an annual trip to Magaluf, but their manager was ahead of Opta Stats and Prozone by roughly 20 years.' It was something that Bassett prided himself on, finding ways to gain an advantage by the means of small margins. 'Billy Beane at Oakland came in with "Moneyball" and all the statistics,' said Bassett. 'We were doing that in 1981.'

For anyone not familiar with the 'Moneyball' story, a small-town baseball team going nowhere and working with only a fraction of the budget compared to that of teams like the New York Yankees and Boston Red Sox, decided to buck the trend and sign players on their statistical analysis rather than the old-fashioned way of recruiting big-name players. The outcome was extraordinary and the team became the first in baseball history to win 20 games in a row. At Wimbledon, there was also talk of Bassett using the club's CCTV footage from the ground to analyse set pieces and goals scored and conceded. This was way before the likes of HUDL and Wyscout began to provide clubs with thousands of hours of video clips to search through. Things like leaving the grass longer in certain areas for the ball to hold up on were all part of the script at Plough Lane and opposition teams hated it.

Bassett was also frugal when it came to finances. Players would ask for an extra fiver a week and would have to flick a coin for the outcome. Contract negotiations for players, including hardman Vinnie Jones, were unconventional. 'During talks with Vinnie, I told him he'd be on £150 a week plus £50 a goal and £50 per appearance in the first team. Then I told him "That's it. See you tomorrow." Vinnie loitered, so I asked "What's up?" He replied something like "Any chance of a signing-on fee?" I told him "No, now fuck off".'

Glynn Hodges came through the youth team at Wimbledon and was signed by Bassett at both Watford and then Sheffield United. Hodges knew that the manager's style of play was often frowned upon and slaughtered by the press but that it was effective. It was direct but with a purpose. 'Your first target would be a long ball from your final third to their final third. I don't know if these are the correct figures,' said Hodges. 'But you had to hit that 100 times and if the winger collected it 40 times and he would get in 12 crosses and from that you would score two goals. This is how it was sold to us. It was a science that worked. We had to play that way and that was how we won games.'

Bassett trained the players hard, ensuring that he left no stone unturned in between matches. 'We trained longer than clubs do today,' said midfielder Wally Downes. 'We worked on 11 v 11. This can be stop-start, with the coach driving home his points, but Harry was a smart teacher and used to build up the sessions, culminating in a game that could flow with the information still fresh.' There was also the dreaded 'Harryball' for the players to navigate. 'I invented Harryball,' said Bassett. 'A player would have to dribble through several grids with the ball and the rules were there were no rules. That caused a few skirmishes. I would also call them in for Sunday training. We had some laughs but when we were working, we were fucking working.'

With his Sheffield United team now sitting in the Third Division, Bassett set about changing not only his squad but also his backroom staff in a bid to stop the rot. The move worked wonders as the team gained promotion at the first attempt. The Blades claimed second spot on goal difference, ensuring that Bassett had achieved an impressive fifth promotion in nine years as a manager. And the journey didn't stop there. Sheffield United set about the Second Division in exactly the same style, despite facing the powerhouses of the other Uniteds, Leeds and Newcastle. And then, of course, there was this FA Cup run woven in with that.

Sheffield United had comfortably dispatched Bournemouth 2-0 in the third round at Bramall Lane and the draw for round four pitched Bassett against the club with whom he had had a brief flirtation before being dismissed. Funny how football works sometimes. The Blades would face a Watford side who, just 18 months earlier, had had 'Harry' in their dugout. Bassett was determined to show his old employers what they were missing out on. A 1-1 draw at home meant the teams would have to go again but Sheffield United took care of business in the replay and left Vicarage Road with a 2-1 win. The fifth round saw an all-Yorkshire clash and this time the Blades needed two replays to eventually squeeze past Barnsley. After a 2-2 draw at Bramall Lane was followed by a 0-0 at Oakwell, they finally made it through with a 1-0 win.

'I must say I had my doubts about Dave coming here,' said Derek Dooley, Sheffield United's chairman. 'I wondered how Sheffield people would take to this cheeky chappy. But he's been marvellous. He's really involved himself in the city.'

You may be wondering about the love-in for Dave Bassett here. I am merely pointing out that, while United had again been drawn against a lower division team, the opposition were certainly capable of performing an upset, as were Hereford and Newcastle United before them. All of the clubs United faced had FA Cup heritage and both Sheffield United and Newcastle had been in the top flight, even if the Blades' absence had been a little more prolonged. Now, their reward for their hard work under Bassett was a televised fixture on 11 March against Alex Ferguson's Manchester United.

The Red Devils were on the crest of a wave following the 3-2 win over Newcastle but, as night follows day, another poor performance in the league in their next fixture brought doubts yet again on the direction the team was travelling in. The 1-0 defeat to Chelsea at Stamford Bridge was a case of 'after the Lord Mayor's Show' following the positive performance on Tyneside. United had slipped back into 16th position and were yet again glancing over their shoulders towards the bottom three. As March arrived, heralding the advent of spring and a change in the seasons, United's form was still, at best, erratic.

A week later and suddenly there was renewed hope again that things were changing for the better as Luton Town came to Old Trafford and left with a walloping. As a football fan, it's the eternal hope that eventually kills you when following your team. Brian McClair opened the scoring after a neat one-two found its way back to the feet of the Scot. Then, in the 33rd minute, a long diagonal ball from Martin to McClair on the right flank was controlled and driven across the 18-yard box for Hughes to sweep home and double the lead. On the stroke of half-time, Danny Wallace made it three to cap off a scintillating first 45 minutes for the hosts. A low Mike Phelan cross was slammed home by Wallace, who was in acres of space at the far post, finishing with aplomb. Robins rounded off the scoring with a fine left-footed strike after Ince had stolen the ball in midfield, played an exquisite one-two with Hughes and then slid the ball into the path of the forward to complete an impressive 4-1 win for Ferguson's men. Despite taking all three points, United stayed cemented in 16th place, with the break of the FA Cup coming at a good or bad time, depending on where your priorities lay.

And so, on to the last eight of the cup, with Dave Bassett's Sheffield United standing in Ferguson's way of reaching the semi-final. It was yet another away trip and one fondly remembered by United fans Adam Moloney and Jon Bailey. 'I was studying at Manchester Polytechnic at the time and managed to find myself in a house of four United fans,' said Moloney. 'We tried to get to every game that season and I seem to remember this was a Sunday lunchtime kick-off and the game was on TV. Doesn't sound like much of a big deal now but there weren't that many games on TV back then. One of the lads had a car, so we made our way across the Pennines for the game and we had the whole of one end at Bramall Lane. We'd been terrible in the league but we felt like something was happening in the cup that year from the moment Mark Robins scored away at Nottingham Forest.'

Jon Bailey had a similar recollection in regard to the mood at the time, although his trip to Bramall Lane was a little livelier. 'The season was pretty awful bar this cup run,' he said. 'Our local supporters branch [Nantwich & Crewe] was set up in the September of 1989, so was relatively new, but we took a full 50-seater coach to every cup match, something you couldn't do these days with the restrictions on ticket allocations. I'd always enjoyed going to Sheffield Wednesday to see us play but this was our first trip to Bramall Lane since 1975, so it was one to tick off. Another Sunday game away from home and a 12.30pm kick-off meant an early start. I was 17 at the time, so wasn't a big drinker, and the previous round had seen me puke into a plastic bag after necking a two-litre bottle of Strongbow on the way to Newcastle and I got plenty of stick from the older lads, so decided to stay sober for this journey.'

Bailey may not have felt the best on his return from Newcastle but having the result in his back pocket would certainly have helped his mood. 'Tickets were handed out on the coach from Andy,' said Bailey. 'He did a great job of getting tickets and usually didn't mind us playing up and drinking. I got a terrace ticket but afterwards wished I'd got a seat. We arrived at our drop-off point but the pubs outside the ground weren't so welcoming, so we went straight in. You had a choice in that terrace – stand in the corner for a decent view or behind the goal. The view was awful, as the fence was massive and there were huge girders that held up the stand above. I wanted to be behind the goal for the atmosphere but was right up against one of the fences.

'The ground was filling up when I noticed in their Kop a group of fans in the bottom right-hand corner keeping away from the rest. Straight away I said "They're all Reds". It was a similar story at Hillsborough the previous season – get in their end and hopefully not get chucked out and get put in our end. The police noticed them, too, and before anything kicked off, they were led out past us and into an empty pen between us and their vocal lot down the side. The Yorkshiremen weren't happy and kicked off a bit but nothing too serious.'

Leighton, Anderson, Martin, Bruce, Pallister, Phelan, Ince, McClair, Wallace, Hughes, and Robins were given the nod by the manager, with the men in all white having what we would imagine would have been only one instruction on the day – don't get beaten. United would certainly have fancied their chances taking lower league opposition back to Old Trafford and the message would have been just to stay in the tie at all costs. On a bright but windy day in Yorkshire, United took the lead on the half-hour after a contentious decision to award the visitors a corner came back to bite the hosts on the proverbial. Wallace played in the corner kick and it was flicked on at the near post to the unmarked McClair, who headed home after his initial header came back off the crossbar.

It was a lead that Ferguson's men held at the interval and one that looked like it had been doubled when McClair raced through the inside-right channel to play a lovely square ball across goal for Mark Robins to fire home but the linesman had other ideas, raising his flag for an offside decision. 'Alex Ferguson has been on his feet more than he's been sitting down in this half,' claimed the commentator, and he had good reason, too, with United holding such a slender advantage. The manager must have been holding his breath as, in the dying moments of the match, Jim Leighton pulled off a double save from Tony Agana, with the forward hitting his first shot straight at the United custodian before scuffing the rebound into the arms of a very thankful Leighton. Agana had been deadly in front of goal for the Blades over the last couple of seasons but his ice-cold finishing deserted him when he needed it the most.

The referee signalled the end of the contest and, yet again, United had squeezed through by the barest of margins. Moloney and Bailey had matching reviews on a game that was dour in comparison to the bright sunshine. 'Sheffield United was a scrappy 1-0 away win but we'd take any kind of win at that stage,' remembers Moloney. 'It was a pretty forgettable game. It was a very windy day and the football from both teams was poor. However, the result was the only thing that mattered.' That sentiment was echoed by Bailey. 'I can't really remember much to get excited about other than it was a big pitch and the weather was decent. I think the game itself was scrappy. We were crap this season but managed great wins in the cup. Anyway, we had won 1-0, so we made it through to the next round and to an FA Cup semi-final. Happy days! That was an occasion where I had a few beers … no Strongbow though!'

With the semi-finals played at a neutral venue, the team would again be boarding a coach, this time making the short trip across town to Manchester City's Maine Road ground to play for a place in the FA Cup Final. The last time Ferguson's men had rocked up at City's home, they were sent back across Manchester with their tails firmly between their legs. This time, Ferguson was hoping for a more positive outcome. But there was still work to do in the league to preserve the team's First Division status as we entered the business end of the season.

FA Cup Semi-Final – Oldham, Kick 'em, Beat them

Venue: Maine Road
Date: 8 April 1990
Attendance: 44,026

JUST THREE days after the FA Cup tie at Bramall Lane, Everton headed to Old Trafford looking to add to Ferguson's woes in the league. Mike Duxbury replaced Viv Anderson in the only change for United, who were still missing the heartbeat of the team in Bryan Robson, as well as summer signing Neil Webb. The visitors should have taken the lead and were a whisker away when a Tony Cottee strike flashed across Jim Leighton's goal and rebounded back off the foot of the far post. It was a real let-off for United, who had begun the match in sluggish fashion, and the Toffees should have made them pay after a prolonged period of pressure that nearly culminated in the opening goal.

Mark Hughes then came close for Ferguson's men after a driving run from McClair released him down the right-hand side of the penalty area. United's No.10 swiftly moved inside his marker and unleashed a fierce left-footed drive but Neville Southall in the visitors' goal was equal to it. Into the second half and it was that man Southall again who denied United, this time saving smartly at the feet of Mark Robins following a melee in the Everton box. Then, United thought they had found a way through when McClair's delicious chip looked to have beaten Southall, only for the keeper to stretch out his fingertips to claw away the Scot's cheeky effort. The ball was still live and fell on to the head of Robins, who could only watch his reaction header fall agonisingly the wrong side of the post.

Then, in the dying seconds, a loose pass back to his defence from Everton's former United hero, Norman Whiteside, was picked up by McClair but his quickfire shot was smothered by man of the match Southall to ensure that the contest ended 0-0, with both teams picking up a well-earned point. The games were coming thick and fast now. Just a few days later, fellow Scousers Liverpool took the short journey to M16 but this time the visitors would leave with all three points as Kenny Dalglish's men won 2-1 and United put in a whimper of a performance.

A fourth match in ten days saw Ferguson and his men head back to Sheffield, this time to take on Wednesday at Hillsborough, where yet again United failed to find the back of the net and were packed off back to Old Trafford with a 1-0 loss against the Owls. Despite only one win in five league matches, United remained in 16th position, still sitting precariously above the relegation zone, but the FA Cup run to the semi-finals had seemingly meant that the manager's job was still cast iron. Just as it looked as if the fixture congestion from the cup was catching up with them, United travelled to The Dell to face Southampton and dug out a performance to lift the mood around the place.

Two significant names on the teamsheet seemed to lift the spirits of the players as Neil Webb and Colin Gibson, who had been missing for seven months and two years respectively, returned to bolster the squad at a vital time in the calendar. And it was Gibson who opened the scoring on his comeback with a fierce left-footed strike from outside the box that flew into the bottom right-hand corner. Mark Hughes had crossed into the Saints box but it was deflected away to safety – or so everyone thought. In fact, it fell beautifully for the left-back to hammer home United's opener. It had been a tough couple of seasons for Gibson, who had been ravaged by injuries, forcing the manager to switch Lee Martin to the other side as cover.

With the game ebbing away from the home side, United doubled the lead with just two minutes remaining to seal a much-needed victory on the road. Mark Robins's late effort, following a save from the Southampton keeper that was only palmed out to the side, was enough to put smiles back on the faces of the lads as they boarded the bus home from the south coast. A week later and three more points were in the bag as United scored three without reply at home to Coventry City. Midway through the first half, United broke the deadlock when a tenacious Paul Ince nicked the ball away from an opposition midfielder before releasing a nice pass into Brian McClair. The Scot slid in Hughes to fire a low, left-footed shot past Steve Ogrizovic in the Sky Blues' goal.

Moments later and Hughes was at it again, this time collecting a high, looping pass from Webb on his chest before firing in his second of the match. What was even more impressive than the opening 36 minutes was the fact that Webb seemed to have fully overcome the troublesome Achilles injury that had kept him out for so long. With just a few minutes left on the clock, substitute Mark Robins sealed a comprehensive win for Ferguson's men to round off a fantastic week in result terms. It was the first time the team had won back-to-back league games since early November, some 18 matches ago. United remained in 16th position but those six points gave them a little breathing space as the FA Cup semi-final loomed large.

When two ex-professional footballers dug their hands into a velvet bag to make the draw for the final four of the competition a week or so earlier, Alex Ferguson, as well as all the United fans around the world, must have thought their Christmases had come all at once when the balls were plucked out to reveal that the Red Devils had again dodged the bullet of Liverpool – and even First Division Crystal Palace for that matter – as they were pitted against lower league opposition again. United had been drawn to play Oldham Athletic, who were a Second Division side at the time, and it was United's fourth favourable tie in a row. Now, all eyes were looking towards a Liverpool-United final. As mentioned previously, Liverpool had walloped Palace 9-0 earlier in the season, so were huge favourites to navigate their way to the final. As a football fan, you always breathe a sigh of relief when your team are drawn against opposition from a lower division but it's by no means a gimme.

As I write this chapter, Oldham Athletic are preparing to face Altrincham on Saturday, 31 August 2024 in a National League fixture (the Vauxhall Conference in old money) in the fifth tier of English football. The Latics have fallen far from grace and in spectacular style since the inception of the Premier League in 1992/93 when Oldham were founder members before their relegation two seasons later. Over the next 30 seasons the club would jolt from manager to manager, owner to owner and, inevitably, division to division before eventually tumbling out of the Football League and into the non-league pyramid at the end of the 2021/22 campaign. Those troubles were in the future, though. This was the beginning of a golden period in the club's history.

Joe Royle was in charge of the Latics during the 1989/90 season and was spearheading what looked like a promotion charge. Oldham fan Dan Turner wrote about his memories of that season for *When Saturday Comes*. 'We started season 1989/90 with four winless games and faded at the end to miss the Second Division play-offs but in the middle was an odyssey of enlightenment, free-flowing Brazilian(ish) football and merciless giganticide,' he said. 'Beating Leeds in those days was routine but never less than hugely satisfying. In fact, it was actually very funny, because the players who frequently proved the difference between the two sides were the very ones we'd nicked from Elland Road for peanuts. Arsenal were sent packing, with the Chaddy End scarcely able to believe it was chanting "easy, easy" at the humiliated league champions. Southampton found AstroTurf and the Oldham monsoon season all just a little bit too much. We toyed with Everton for three games before sending them on their way. Aston Villa needed only the one. By the time we'd got to West Ham, we'd all got a bit blasé. So, our genial Scouse manager woke us from our complacency by deciding that the right formation for a League Cup semi-final was 3-2-5. But we needn't have worried – it resulted in a 6-0 first-leg victory that still causes shivers among the Upton Park faithful, so I'm told.'

Oh, by the way, do you remember earlier when I mentioned the 'plastic pitch' of Luton Town? Well, back in the early 1980s, there were a handful of clubs in England who adopted a different style of playing surface to the more conventional offering of grass. Luton Town, Oldham Athletic, Queens Park Rangers and Preston North End all tried the more flamboyant concept of the 'plastic' pitch. Now, for those of you wondering what difference the pitch might make, let me explain. If you go to a Premier League ground on the last day of the season nowadays, you will notice a pitch in pristine condition, akin to the opening weekend in August. They are a mixture of grass and artificial fibres that are woven together to protect against wear and tear. Decades earlier, however, even the biggest clubs in the world would have areas with little to no grass as we headed into the winter months, most noticeably in the centre circle and both six-yard boxes. Now, pitches look like billiard tables all season long.

In an attempt to buck the trend, the four aforementioned clubs embarked on what can only be described as a whole new world in footballing terms, as first Queens Park Rangers ripped up their ailing grass surface and replaced it with an Omni-Turf style of AstroTurf that was quickly universally labelled a 'plastic pitch'. Delegates from Loftus Road had headed west to our chums across the Atlantic to carry out some research on pitches that had been in place there since the 1960s. They liked what they saw and moved quickly to install one of their own. Success followed for the Hoops but with every success in a certain field comes a copycat mentality from others looking to imitate and improve on your achievement.

Steven Scragg, writing for *These Football Times*, researched the origins of the surface and wrote: 'AstroTurf and big-time sport had initially joined together in 1966 at the Houston Astrodome. After a year of trying to make grass grow indoors, the owners of the stadium opted for an alternative. While the AstroTurf surface didn't meet with universal approval, it was very effective and of a lower maintenance level when it came to its upkeep. New artificial pitches popped up all across North America in no time at all and in a number of different sports. Some people loved the new surfaces, while others were far from impressed. Baseball star Dick Allen declared "If a horse won't eat it, I don't want to play on it".'

But it wasn't all plain sailing for QPR. Within days of installing their new carpet-like surface, someone broke in and graffitied on it, 'PERRY BUCKLAND IS INNOCENT. Well, at least someone with a tin of whitewash and a few hours to spare on Christmas Day 1981 thought so,' wrote Scragg. 'It was a proclamation that was daubed on to Queens Park Rangers' pitch prior to their Boxing Day Division Two derby encounter with Chelsea, a game that took place on QPR's recently installed, groundbreaking and often derided artificial pitch.'

Despite this hiccup for QPR, Oldham, who at the time were a middle-of-the-road Division Two club, decided to follow suit and install a nice shiny new 'plastic' pitch of their own. Cue an impressive 32-match unbeaten run, including some impressive FA Cup giant-killings. Alex Ferguson was hoping that he wasn't about to be added to this list.

* * *

Pete Boyle has followed Manchester United home and away for years. He, too, remembers the uncertainty around the club at the time, as well as the unbridled joy that the FA Cup was bringing at a time when both the football club and the manager needed it the most. 'My first game was November 1974 when I was just four years old,' said Boyle. 'We played Aston Villa. I remember going quite a bit around that time and we only lost twice, the first against Tottenham Hotspur, where we were 2-0 up at half-time and we lost 3-2. We lost to Everton 3-0 in the League Cup and being so young, I found it really hard to take. My dad took me then and the 1976/77 season was when I really started coming of age, going to most of the cup run that season.'

The cup run in question was that of United returning to the final following the heartbreaking defeat to Division Two Southampton a season earlier. 'I went to Queens Park Rangers in the fourth round, the Southampton replay, Villa in quarter-final and Leeds United in the semi-final, where the United fans had three-quarters of Hillsborough, and then the final itself against Liverpool. It was one of the lasting memories of me and my dad, which gets me quite teary-eyed every time I watch that game. My support has never wavered through thick and thin and I have seen some good years but also some pretty bad years.'

Sunday, 8 April 1990 was about to go down in the record books. Not only were the BBC showing both FA Cup semi-final matches live for the first time in history but they were to be beamed into our homes one after the other, with only the *EastEnders Omnibus* as the filling in this fine footballing sandwich. 'It is a poor and unimaginative idea,' wrote Peter Corrigan in *The Observer*. 'The danger of the entire exercise being a drag is not all that slim.' Liverpool versus Crystal Palace was to kick off at noon and Manchester United-Oldham Athletic would follow at 3.30pm. 'Pete and the market traders rally to protect their future while Diane finds that the past won't go away,' was how the *Radio Times* described the goings-on in Albert Square that particular week. Mind you, the greatest drama that day didn't occur in the Queen Vic or on Pete's market stall. Oh, no! That was saved for Villa Park and then Maine Road.

Kenny Dalglish's all-conquering Liverpool team were seemingly heading towards their 18th league title, while Steve Coppell's Crystal Palace were fighting for their lives at the wrong end of the table. It was a game that was seen as a foregone conclusion, with the current FA Cup holders only having to turn up to ensure a place back in the Wembley showpiece. And when Liverpool took a 1-0 lead through Ian Rush on 14 minutes, many armchair viewers could have been forgiven for thinking the result was inevitable and flicking through the other three channels while waiting for their weekly trip to Albert Square. But, in true *EastEnders* fashion, there was to be a huge plot twist in this cup tie.

Just 16 seconds into the second half, Mark Bright grabbed an equaliser after a barnstorming run from right-back John Pemberton caused panic in the Liverpool defence. In the 70th minute, the game turned on its head when Gary O'Reilly put Palace ahead to set up a tantalising last 20 minutes. But the drama was only just beginning. With only ten minutes left on the clock, Steve McMahon levelled the tie following a neat free-kick routine and when John Barnes scored from the penalty spot with five minutes remaining, it looked like the footballing equilibrium had been restored. That was until Andy Gray pounced on a bobbling ball to head it past a swamp of Liverpool defenders and send the tie into extra time, with anyone tuning in for the start of *EastEnders* witnessing a marvellous 30 minutes of football instead.

Liverpool were on the ropes, knackered and weary, while Palace looked energised as the teams headed back out on to the pitch. The men from Merseyside, wearing an all-silver kit, had been struggling all afternoon with the Eagles' set-piece routines and it was a corner that would eventually be their undoing. Palace won one at the Holte End and the ball was swung into the Liverpool box. Dalglish's men were unable to clear and Alan Pardew saw his opportunity, arriving late to score at the far post after a near post flick-on to send the Palace fans into raptures; 4-3 Palace. Wave after wave of Liverpool attacks were seen off by a resilient Palace rearguard until time eventually ran out for the holders and Coppell's men had upset the odds and reached the Wembley final.

The first serving had been an absolute cracker. It was end-to-end like a basketball game. 'What I can remember about the semi-final was, well, the Liverpool v Crystal Palace game, we were watching it in the Friendship pub on the television and we were all expecting Liverpool to win but little did we know what was about to happen as they lost and we didn't know it then but they then go on for 30 years without winning another league title,' smiled Boyle. 'We made our way to the ground and a few of us ended up in the Oldham end in Platt Lane. I'm not too sure how that came about but we were jubilant, thinking we could win it. Yes! Liverpool were out. We would have turned up at Wembley against Liverpool if we had both made the final, even though we would have been underdogs again.'

Fellow United fan David Leach gave his recollection of the build-up to the match. 'I remember it was a cracking day, hot and sunny,' said Leach. 'It was my first semi-final watching United and the FA Cup was massive in those days. I watched the first half of Palace v Liverpool on TV at home. Half-time and it was time to meet mates and set off to Maine Road. Got the bus down Oldham Road into Piccadilly, then jumped on the football special buses laid on to take Reds to the hovel. As we got off the bus and walked to the ground, the news filtered through that Crystal Palace had beaten Liverpool 4-3 and the atmosphere was significantly lifted even further. Surely the cup was ours?' The pre-match talk was mixed with people summarising the events that had unfolded beforehand at Villa Park and those that were about to come at Maine Road.

The BBC tried to flower up the occasion as much as possible but they had the unenviable task of trying to bring people back to earth following the earlier game, which had been from another planet. 'Hello and welcome to live coverage of After the Lord Mayor's Show,' proclaimed Des Lynam. 'The greatest match in FA Cup history ended a few minutes ago, with Crystal Palace beating Liverpool 4-3 in an absolute astonisher at Villa Park. Spare a thought for the players of Oldham and Manchester United, who have the impossible task of trying to replicate the drama when they kick off at Maine Road. United, meanwhile, are in a bit of a purple patch … they have won two league games in a row for only the second time in 14 months and are now five points above the relegation zone. Neil Webb and Bryan

Robson are both back after long-term injuries. The odds have tipped in United's favour.'

The Guardian chief football correspondent David Lacey's scorecast was 3-1 United after extra time. He wrote: 'There's another reason why so many people fancy United today: the match is being played on grass. All Oldham's giant-killings have taken place on the plastic pitch at Boundary Park, which is also where they've picked up 42 of their 57 league points. But they also played well in drawing away to Everton and Southampton before finishing them off in a replay and Graham Taylor and George Graham – whose Villa and Arsenal sides were hammered at Boundary Park – both said it had diddly squat to do with the pitch. When Oldham thrashed Aston Villa, the Division One leaders, in the quarter-final last month, the smart money was on them beating United. But things have changed since then. Oldham have lost their last three games without scoring a goal and are down to ninth place in Division Two, though they do have two games in hand on all the sides above them. It looks like their season of derring-do – this is their 54th game, with at least another ten to come – might be catching up with them.' United fans at Maine Road would have been buoyed even further by the team news being read over the Tannoy that a certain Bryan Robson was about to make his first start since Christmas. A huge cheer rang around the ground when it was announced that United's talisman was, in fact, starting. Of course, these days team news is readily available an hour before kick-off through social media and team's websites but back then you had to wait to hear it from the stadium announcer or for the two line-ups to be displayed on the stadium scoreboard. It was certainly a gamble for the manager to bring back his captain, having not played any first-team football for such a long period but it was one he was certainly willing to take. Leighton, Phelan, Pallister, Bruce, Martin, McClair, Ince, Robson, Gibson, Webb and Hughes were given the task of setting up a final meeting with Crystal Palace.

If Ferguson or anyone watching wondered if Robson was going to feel his way into the match, having been out for so long, they got their answer with just three minutes on the clock when he introduced himself to Andy Ritchie with a ferocious man-and-ball tackle. 'The ball must have squealed!' said the BBC commentator Barry Davies, wincing as he spoke. Despite the rallying call from United's No.7, Oldham would take the lead as early as the sixth minute, with Earl Barrett tapping into an empty net following a corner which Jim Leighton should have dealt with better. He was pinned by Andy Holden and was then left stranded as the Latics took the lead. It was the first time during this cup run that United had trailed – and thoughts of the last visit to Maine Road were still firmly in people's minds.

United struggled early on to get a foothold in the game and failed to find any rhythm, with Webb a passenger and Hughes only finding offside positions. In fact, both teams were being caught offside far too often in a game being played at 100mph. 'If there's a word that would sum up Manchester United's performance so far, it is "uncomfortable". All over the pitch, they are not enjoying what they are being asked to do,' said Davies. The Division Two side were fighting for every ball and winning most of the duels around the pitch but there was still plenty of time left for Ferguson's men to show that they, too, had some fight.

And it was that spirit that brought about the equaliser on the half-hour as a fantastic sliding tackle by Bruce on the halfway line saw the ball make its way to Webb, who took one touch and slid a beautiful through ball to Robson. The skipper, who had been stuck on his backside just seconds earlier following a challenge by Mike Milligan, ran through and slid the ball past Hallworth in the Oldham goal to bring the sides level. It was the measure of the man that he would drag the team kicking and screaming back into the match, as he had done so many times during the last nine years. Ferguson would have been thrilled that the two players he gambled on, Webb and Robson, had combined for the goal. It was a really good ball from Webb, a serene touch of class in this frenetic game. Including a replay, it was the fourth semi-final running in which Robson had found the net.

As the game edged towards half-time, both sides went close. First, Paul Ince cleared an Oldham effort off the goal line and then Oldham full-back Denis Irwin (he looks a good player, we thought!) blocked well when Robson looked to double his tally for the day. After the late near misses, the teams headed down the tunnel at 1-1. United began the second period as they had started the first, in sluggish mood, looking more like a team who were desperate not to lose rather than one who were expecting to win. Oldham could smell blood and crashed into every tackle like their lives depended on it, most notably when Ince and Ritchie had a coming-together. They squared up to one another before Ince playfully patted Ritchie on his bald head as he jogged away.

Hughes's attempted through pass to McClair was blocked by Barrett. The ball ran loose between them, at which point Hughes booted Barrett straight up in the air. That was a tackle of pure frustration, although it would probably be generous to call it a tackle. It was a hack, essentially, and it was slightly surprising Hughes didn't have his name taken by referee Joe Worrall. With United finding it difficult to gain control, Oldham nearly took the lead on the hour when a low drive from Marshall was well saved by Leighton, who beat away the Oldham striker's shot.

With just 20 minutes left to play, Robson was withdrawn from the action to be replaced by Danny Wallace. United's skipper had run himself into the ground. He had only been about 50 per cent match fit but that hadn't fazed him – he just wanted to be out there. Within a couple of minutes of the substitution, the incoming Wallace made an immediate impact on the match. Receiving a throw-in in the right-hand corner, United's No.12 spun his man and sliced a left-footed cross to the far side of the penalty area. The ball was nodded back towards the six-yard box and Neil Webb, who had ghosted in between the two centre-backs, jumped with keeper Hallworth as the ball looped high into the afternoon sun. The ball seemed to glance off the top of the United midfielder's head and it looped over the stranded keeper and into the empty net. United had taken the lead for the first time in the match and had Wembley firmly in their sights with just 17 minutes remaining. It certainly wasn't going to be a contender for any goal of the month awards but Webb and United couldn't care less. Hallworth must have thought he could get to the cross first but Webb got there a split second before him and was able, more by luck than judgment, to guide his effort into the Oldham net. Hallworth looked as bemused as the goalscorer, who did a full 360 before realising where the ball had gone, then ran towards the red army behind the Latics' goal. The decision to start both midfielders despite long injury lays-offs was paying Ferguson back with dividends.

The joy, however, would last only four minutes. A Bruce clearance into the corner for a throw-in looked to have nullified the Oldham pressure but a neat one-two between Irwin and Rick Holden resulted in a cross that seemed to take a flick on its way through before Marshall volleyed it back in the direction in came from to and into the far bottom-right corner. Leighton could only stand and wave it past as Oldham's No.9 with the mullet wheeled off in celebration. 'What an unbelievable day this has been,' cried BBC commentator Davies. You just couldn't believe that this game was going to go the distance, like its predecessor a couple of hours earlier, but it did.

'For the second time today, we're going to extra time. So much for After the Lord Mayor's Show – this is the Lord Mayor's Show part two!' claimed the animated Lynam in the BBC studio. The camera cut to the Oldham Athletic bench, where Joe Royle had a huge smile on his face. It wasn't even a forced or nervous smile; he looked like he was having the time of his life. Alex Ferguson, in stark contrast, had the demeanour of a man whose life depended on the next 30 minutes. Maybe it did. Oldham kicked off the first period of extra time but a poor first touch from Ritchie enabled McClair to claim possession. McClair looked up and played a direct through ball into the path of the nimble Wallace, who had cleverly placed himself between both central defenders.

'Useful for Wallace. Test of his pace and now a test of his finish … and … he's equalled them both,' declared Barry Davies. Hallworth rushed out to meet Wallace but the winger scuffed his left-footed effort into the far corner of the net to give United a 3-2 lead. It had been some impact by the substitute, with an assist and a goal already in his cameo appearance. And it looked like it was going to be enough to see off Royle's spirited team. Once again, though, they came back. In the second period of extra time, a free kick from Irwin was only half cleared, falling to the feet of Mark Robins and, instead of trying to keep possession and running down the clock, he gave the ball back to Oldham. Milligan's pass to Marshall found the forward in acres of space down the left-hand side. He looked up and delivered a sublime cross along the floor and there was Roger Palmer to tap home at the far post.

Marshall's cross directly along the six-yard line found what they call the 'corridor of uncertainty' – an area where the ball is slightly out of the reach of the goalkeeper and his defenders, facing their own goal, are too terrified to try and block it for fear of putting the ball into their own net. Marshall's cross evaded the onlooking Leighton, who was in no man's land, and teased both Bruce and Gary Pallister, who could only watch the ball sail past and hope it went across to safety. It didn't. Oldham goal machine Palmer ghosted in unmarked at the back post to bring the sides level at 3-3. 'This is the stuff of schoolboy comics! Marshall into the path of Palmer and Oldham have levelled again. Marvellous stuff,' said Barry Davies.

In the 120th minute and, with one last throw of the dice for United, Webb's lofted pass was headed back infield by Robins towards Hughes in the penalty area. Hughes launched himself towards the bouncing ball and was just beaten to it by Hallworth, who bravely punched clear as he was clattered by United's No.10. 'There's no more fearsome sight at a bouncing ball than Mark Hughes bearing down on you,' remarked BBC co-commentator Trevor Brooking. Oldham looked to rally late on and Ferguson responded by dropping Webb deeper to give extra protection to his backline. United were now playing 4-5-1, Oldham a kind of 3-4-1-2. Is that even a formation? Who knows! It was to Joe Royle, anyway.

As the referee blew time on the second scintillating match of the day, 18,000 Latics fans sang 'We can play on grass as well' as they clapped their heroes off the pitch. The two teams were going to have to do it all again just a few days later. United definitely didn't need a replay, with an already congested tail end of the campaign, but staying in the competition was, of course, a hell of a lot better than crashing out, which could have been the case.

'The contrast between the two managers is stark,' wrote Peter Harthan in *The Guardian*. 'Ferguson has looked out of his depth ever since he came to England from Scottish football and surely won't last long. Royle has a long future and will probably be England manager in time, mark my words.' A bold statement but testament to the feeling at the time around Ferguson's spell at United despite the lifeline that the FA Cup had provided him.

Harthan's article summed up the events of the day perfectly. 'Peep peep! That's it! Joe Royle and Alex Ferguson shake hands, and then Royle puts his arm round Ferguson. There is such generosity of spirit about him and his players; they're the most loveable team in England. Ferguson, meanwhile, has the expression of a man who has just been told his firing squad are stuck in traffic. The teams will be back here on Wednesday night for the replay, which Des Lynam has confirmed will be shown live on *Sportsnight*. For now, let's glory in surely the greatest day in FA Cup history: 13 goals, 13 different goalscorers and two games that will never be forgotten. Those of us who thought that having two live games on the same day was a disastrous idea are about to have a late Sunday dinner of roasted humble pie.

'The success of today's experiment probably means that the FA Cup semi-final double header will become an annual tradition. Who knows? In time, we might even have two league games being televised on the same day. But whatever happens in the future, I doubt we'll ever see a double header as dramatic as this.'

The United-Oldham game was only part of a magnificent weekend of sport. You had the two pulsating semi-final matches that produced 13 goals between them, as well as a giant-killing, with no one really giving Crystal Palace a chance. Not even the most optimistic of diehard Palace fans could have envisaged that result. There was also a record-breaking run at Aintree when amateur jockey Marcus Armytage romped home on Mr Frisk in a time of 8 minutes 47.80 seconds to claim the Grand National. It is a record that still stands to this day. Nick Faldo claimed a Masters victory at Augusta to round off a fantastic weekend's viewing.

For United, there was still work to be done. Ferguson replaced Colin Gibson with the impressive Danny Wallace in the only change for United as the two teams faced off just three days later. Again, Maine Road was the venue as United, in red, and Oldham, in blue, took to the field to do battle once more. This time, there would be an outcome by the end of the evening, whatever the result, with a penalty shoot-out to be held if required. It was a pretty tepid first half, as both teams looked leggy from Sunday's encounter. However, just five minutes after the restart, Brian McClair gave Ferguson's men the lead.

Wallace, who had tormented the Latics when coming on in the first game, drove down the left flank after fine work by Bryan Robson to win back the ball in true combative style. As Wallace ran towards the left byline, Robson was just inside of him, screaming for the ball to be returned, but Wallace had noticed that Robson had attracted a couple of Oldham defenders and that this, in turn, had opened a gaping hole inside the Latics penalty area. Wallace drove a low, left-footed cross into the area and it took a small deflection off Nick Henry's ankle, evaded all the men in blue and wound up at the back post, where McClair couldn't believe his luck. United's No.9 sidefooted the ball into the empty net and ran towards the corner flag with his fist clenched in celebration.

If the last match was anything to go by, then Oldham were far from done and, with less than ten minutes remaining, they hit back with an equaliser. Joe Royle's men were certainly not going down without a fight. United had failed to clear their lines when Irwin's low cross was met with a diving header by Ince, only for the ball to return to Irwin. The full-back played a sideways pass to Rick Holden just inside the right-hand side of the penalty area and his first-time cross was deflected back to him, amidst appeals for handball that were waved away by the referee. Holden again crossed but this time it was into a dangerous area and when Neil Webb's glancing header was then missed by Mike Phelan, Andy Ritchie ghosted in at the far stick and rammed the ball past Jim Leighton and into the roof of the net.

When the referee signalled that normal time had been completed, for the second match running an additional 30 minutes were going to be staged. Both teams looked dead on their feet as their respective managers tried to rouse them for one final push. The quality had gone as legs grew heavy. Now, it was a case of who had the most heart to get over the line. The first 15 minutes whizzed past with little to no action of note but, with just six minutes left, Mark Robins came up trumps for Alex Ferguson. Webb's clever through ball set away Mike Phelan down the right flank and he marauded his way past his marker before sliding the ball inside Earl Barrett just outside the penalty area for Robins, who took two touches, steadied himself and slotted the ball past Hallworth into the far left-hand corner.

This time, there was no way back for Royle's side and the referee blew his whistle to signal the end of a pulsating semi-final. Ferguson hugged Robins and Lee Sharpe before shaking the hand of his counterpart in the opposite dug-out. A few fans invaded the pitch and hoisted goalscorer Robins on to their shoulders, parading him around like their new messiah – and who could blame them? United were heading back to Wembley for the first time in five years. It was a huge relief for the manager, who had seemingly felt the noose tighten around his neck each week, only to feel it loosen again as each round of the FA Cup was successfully navigated.

Crystal Palace at the home of football, under the twin towers, awaited Ferguson and his men. But first there were six more 'cup finals' left to play, with points still needed to ensure that the club would still be a First Division outfit at the start of the 1990/91 season. For now, the success of the FA Cup semi-final and the excitement over the upcoming showpiece would have to be put on the backburner. There was a job to do. Focus was switched back to the bread and butter of the league and Ferguson knew that it was time for his team to dig out results.

Oh, and for those of you curious about the Oldham Athletic versus Altrincham result on 31 August 2024 in the Vanarama National League … it was a 1-1 draw.

Onwards and Upwards

FOLLOWING THE two semi-final matches against Oldham Athletic, it meant that United were now unbeaten in four games in all competitions, the team's best run of the season to date. A trip to Loftus Road in west London on 14 April was up next for Ferguson's men, who were looking to make it three wins out of three in the league and hammer a bigger wedge between themselves and the relegation places. On-loan goalkeeper Les Sealey, who had signed for the club as cover for Jim Leighton a few months earlier, was to make his first start of the season because the Scot wasn't passed fit. Sealey, Phelan, Martin, Pallister, Bruce, Robson, Ince, Webb, Wallace, McClair and Hughes were charged with keeping the run going.

It was the hosts who took the lead in the opening 45 minutes. In the 33rd minute, Justin Channing gave the Hoops the advantage, firing past the debutant Sealey, who could do little to stop the home side from scoring. Early into the second period and Ferguson looked to his goalscoring hero from a few days earlier, sending on Mark Robins to try and provide a spark in United's attack. Within eight minutes of his arrival, he did just that. It had been wave after wave of United attacks as the visitors tried to claw their way back into the game and eventually, in the 68th minute, Queens Park Rangers' sturdy defence finally gave way. A ball across the defence eventually found its way to the back post where McClair beat his man and rolled it back across the six-yard box for Robins to slam home from close range. Ferguson's men had their tails up and could smell blood and, more importantly, three precious points. Just six minutes later, they scored again, this time through Neil Webb. United's No.8 started the move by picking the pocket of a Rangers forward and playing a pass to Robson. United's skipper chipped a lovely ball over the home defence for Robins to run on to before beating his man and playing a pass back towards the onrushing Webb, who fired past David Seamen to make it 2-1.

United managed to cling on to the result and it not only ensured that they kept their good run of form going, the win moved Ferguson's men up two places in the table to 14th position. It was the first time for seven weeks that the club's position in the table had changed and it gave the team a little breathing space with just five league matches remaining. Three of those remaining fixtures were on home soil and even the most pessimistic of United fans at the time would have backed the team to prevail when playing at Old Trafford. As United prepared for the visit of Aston Villa just a couple of days after the victory at QPR, the manager could, at last, start looking upwards rather than over his shoulder at the relegation pack. It was a congested fixture list around that Easter period and this created concern over player workloads, especially with the heart of the midfield, Robson and Webb, having had so much time out and having had to rush back to get stuck into the big games. To be honest, at this stage of the campaign, every single game was a big game. Sealey kept his place in goal in place of the injured Leighton but there were two changes in personnel, with Colin Gibson and Viv Anderson replacing Lee Martin and Paul Ince. The manager was having to shuffle his pack as the games came thick and fast and human nature would suggest that, despite feeling the team were safe from relegation, he would have one eye on the FA Cup Final the following month.

Aston Villa seemed to navigate the opening 20 minutes of the fixture well, including keeping the near 45,000 supporters inside Old Trafford quiet. That was until midway through the first half when Mark Robins found a breakthrough to give the hosts the impetus to go on and win the match against Graham Taylor's title contenders. Danny Wallace collected the ball on the right flank and whipped in a beautiful low cross for Robins to score with a cracking diving header. The pitch might have resembled a ploughed field but United were passing the ball around with a real vigour, playing with ease and confidence. It's amazing what a couple of wins can do for a team's confidence.

Then, on the stroke of half-time, Robins doubled the lead, scoring both his and United's second of the afternoon. Webb picked up a loose ball on the edge of United's penalty area and played a forward pass to Hughes on the edge of the centre circle. The Welshman spun his marker, making space for himself to look up and beat his nearest man. As he made his way down the right touchline, the Aston Villa midfield was nowhere to be seen and, with a slide rule pass, Hughes picked out the run of Robins. The young forward, who was, bizarrely, wearing the No.4 shirt, produced a first-time finish with the outside of his left foot from just inside Villa's 18-yard box, the shot flying into the top corner past the stranded Nigel Spink. Ferguson's men held on and not only managed to keep a clean sheet but also dispelled any more talk of relegation. The Red Devils had now steered themselves well clear of the danger zone.

The team had climbed the table to the heady heights of 13th, their highest league position since the Christmas period, but produced an abject performance a week later at White Hart Lane when a 2-1 defeat to Tottenham Hotspur derailed the momentum that had been built up by Ferguson's men. With the pressures of trying to stay up in the league, coupled with the FA Cup run, the players could maybe have been forgiven for possibly running on empty at this point. The players would also not haver wanted to have risked an injury and potentially missing the big one against Crystal Palace. Gary Lineker and Paul Gascoigne were on target for Spurs and a Steve Bruce penalty was just a consolation as United tumbled to defeat in north London.

Jim Leighton had returned between the sticks, despite Sealey undertaking an impressive stint as understudy, but it wasn't the last we would see of the cheeky Cockney. A 0-0 draw at home to Wimbledon followed by a 4-0 hammering at Nottingham Forest all but signed off on what was regarded as a poor showing in the league, although not before the Old Trafford faithful got to see their heroes for the final time of the campaign in a 1-0 win over Charlton. A Gary Pallister goal in the 36th minute sealed the victory. He found the net with a fine left-footed strike after defensive partner Bruce saw his header saved. Pallister was in the right place at the right time to lash home from eight yards out and secure three points that meant United would finish in a very disappointing 13th position.

The final table didn't make great reading for the manager. He had spent big money moulding the squad into one he could finally call his own and, by his own admission, they had under-performed. Injuries to his engine room, including star signing Neil Webb, were cited as part of the problem in a season in which United could never quite get going in the league. The team was plagued with inconsistency, which ultimately ended any thoughts of a title run as early as mid-autumn. There were rumblings of discontent in the boardroom and on the terraces but the manager had an ace up his sleeve. And, on 12 May 1990, he was about to show his hand.

FA Cup Final – She Wore, She Wore…

Venue: Wembley Stadium
Date: 12 May 1990
Attendance: 80,000

FATE IN football has a funny way of throwing up circumstances that always bring a little bit of devilment to an occasion. Like an old player coming back to score against you after moving to a new club or a manager getting one over on a team that may have given him the sack. Occasions in football when people get the opportunity to gain the last laugh are more commonplace than you would care to imagine and, of course, that applied to the 1990 FA Cup Final. United were facing Crystal Palace at Wembley – the very team whose Old Trafford victory in December had seen Ferguson face what was, arguably, his darkest hour as Manchester United manager.

Palace, managed by United old boy Steve Coppell, finished on the same points as Ferguson's men in the

First Division table but a couple of positions lower on goal difference. This was largely due to the nine they had conceded at Anfield and the reality was that there wasn't a huge difference between the two sides over the course of a 38-game season. Coppell had been a majestic player for the Red Devils, most notably under Tommy Docherty, with the winger becoming a real favourite of the Stretford End. Signed as a 20-year-old from Tranmere Rovers, Coppell featured more than 300 times in a red shirt, scoring more than 50 times in a career that included winning the 1977 FA Cup.

Despite the anomaly of Palace's 9-0 loss at Liverpool, a season which produced a mid-table finish and a cup final would have been welcomed down in south London. Palace's honours list pales into significance when compared to the trophy haul United have won over the last 100-odd years. Palace's achievements include a Division Two title in 1978/79, a Division Three title in 1920/21 and a couple of Wartime League titles between 1939 and 1941. Sprinkle in the odd Southern Football League title and London Challenge Cup from the beginning of the 1900s and you can gauge the gulf between the two clubs in terms of footballing achievements. Now, please don't think I am looking down my nose at Palace's list of honours; far from it. Some teams have never won anything at all in their history, outside of local competitions. Rochdale, for example, have never won a trophy other than the Lancashire Cup.

History lesson aside, and in this season in particular, you could just about split the two sides with a cigarette paper. Of course, this book has documented the route to the final for Manchester United. A difficult third-round opponent in Nottingham Forest – who could have finished the run before it had even begun – was followed by a trip to Fourth Division Hereford United. Winning that match set up ties against three teams from the Second Division, all of whom were fighting hard for promotion. To top it all off for Alex Ferguson's men, not one match was played at Old Trafford during the cup run. It was a record that stood until the 2018/19 season when Manchester City played every game away from their home ground on the way to reaching the semi-finals. In fact, Manchester United had achieved the feat before back in 1948. United won the FA Cup by beating Aston Villa, Liverpool, Charlton Athletic, Preston, Derby County and Blackpool in the process. All of which were First Division teams at the time. Old Trafford was still being rebuilt following bomb damage during World War Two, so technically they played every game away from home then, too.

The Eagles had faced a similar road to Wembley, avoiding all the big guns until they faced Liverpool in the last four of the competition. They hosted Portsmouth in the third round, winning 2-1. The draw was kind to Palace, rewarding them with another home tie, this time against Huddersfield Town and a 4-0 thumping saw

Coppell's men safely through to round five, where they would face lower league opposition at home once more. It was our aforementioned Lancashire Cup friends, Rochdale, who headed to south London, looking to break their major trophy duck, only to be sent back up the M1 following a 1-0 defeat. A quarter-final tie at Cambridge United presented a potential banana skin but Coppell's men navigated their way out of the Abbey Stadium with another clean sheet and a 1-0 win. This, of course, brought us to the finest footballing day that anyone can care to remember.

The draw for the semi-final stages pitted Crystal Palace against Liverpool and Manchester United against Oldham Athletic, with Palace getting their first real test of the competition. As I mentioned earlier, both matches were played on a Sunday and televised live for the first time and it was Palace who were tasked with kicking off proceedings. A Liverpool fan was stopped for a chat by a reporter on his way into Villa Park and said: 'My prediction? 7-0. I've just been leafing through my official 1990 Liverpool Annual and the double-page spread on the 9-0 is evidence of how this one is going to go.' Confidence was high amongst the men from Merseyside but not so much from the opposition. 'As a Palace fan I don't think we have a hope today,' sighed Sam Smedley. 'No Ian Wright and Alan bloody Pardew starting.' In his pre-match interview, manager Coppell played down his team's chances. 'Of course, we shouldn't have a chance,' he said. 'Deep down, I'm sure the players know they are likely to be beaten, too. But I'm equally sure this will make them play even harder to win.'

Skippers Geoff Thomas and Alan Hansen shook hands before the game began and we were off and running in the first of what were about to become arguably the greatest two semi-final fixtures of all-time. It was a topsy turvy match, swinging one way and then another, with Liverpool leading twice before being pegged back by the sheer resilience of Crystal Palace. Ian Rush going off injured just 30 minutes into the match, having earlier given Liverpool the lead, must have given the Eagles a boost as they chased the game before equalising through Mark Bright. Ray Wilkins, back in the BBC studio with anchor Bob Wilson, was adamant that the tie would go to the form book. 'I think Liverpool have been superior in every department,' he said as the panel reviewed the first 45 minutes of action.

With Bright having equalised just after the restart, Palace took the lead with 20 minutes to go, only for the pendulum to swing back in Liverpool's favour with just moments remaining. That was until a late, late equaliser from Andy Gray meant that an additional 30 minutes had to be played in a bid to separate the sides. Liverpool looked dead on their feet and when Alan Pardew nodded in on 108 minutes, the men dressed in all silver had no reply this time around. I can remember, back then, thinking that this result was huge. After all, Liverpool rarely lost football matches. Little did we know at the time that the trophy machine from Anfield was about to hit the skids.

'Can Manchester United and Oldham follow this?' John Motson wondered on BBC One. 'I'm sure they'll try their best.' And, as we all know now, they sure as hell tried. Kenny Dalglish was bullish in his post-match press conference. 'Football-wise, we were better than they were but they were better organised at set pieces,' said the disgruntled Liverpool gaffer. Coppell was asked about his side's success at set plays. 'I don't think Liverpool are weak at set pieces. But teams know that these are the only occasions when they can be sure of getting in crosses with five or six men in the box.'

It was a fantastic achievement for the Eagles boss but, as he congratulated his players as they walked down the tunnel at Villa Park, he would have been well aware that it could have turned out differently. 'The team with the best players doesn't always win a semi-final,' said Coppell. . 'It's a one-off. Sometimes character, determination, guts and passion are more important than skill. This may sound a horrible thing to say but it's true. I wasn't too worried about being a goal down at half-time. I told the players not to panic and that there was no problem. To be honest, I thought when they went ahead at 3-2, we had blown it and that in extra time both sides had settled for a replay. I was panicking then, because we hadn't rebooked our hotel for midweek! I was convinced the game would be won or lost today.'

Luckily for Palace, they clawed their way to Wembley and didn't have to sleep on the coach if there had been a replay the following Wednesday!

As a kid growing up in the pre-Premier League era, there was something magical about FA Cup Final day. The TV build-up would start in the morning, around 9am, with both BBC and ITV getting in on the act as they showed you footage of the players eating their breakfast and, if you were lucky, you would get a cheeky little interview from a couple of players to really get the juices flowing. Then there would be the coaches driving to Wembley with film crews on them. Imagine that today. You would have the 'Road to Wembley', showing you how both teams got there in fine detail and the songs ... my God, the songs! Crystal Palace's was 'Glad All Over', a song they still use to come out on to the pitch to today. I must admit I secretly like the song and think it's far better than some of the other anthems that teams across the land use. It's catchy.

With Palace's ditty featuring on *Top of the Pops*, it's easy to forget the absolute abomination that was Manchester United's effort. *We Will Stand Together* barely made the top 100. Like United's league performance over that season, the song limped in at number 93 and was in the charts for a grand total of two weeks. Palace, on the other hand, held the bragging rights when it came to making music. Peaking at No.50 and staying in the charts for just over a month gave the Eagles an artistic win. A little psychological advantage they would look to take into their first FA Cup Final in 85 years against a club who were about to embark on their third inside a decade.

And so, on to Wembley. The stadium was to host the first all-seater final – a taste of things to come at grounds around the country after the Taylor Report following the 1989 Hillsborough disaster stipulated that there would be no terraces at major grounds. The home of English football was bathed in sunshine on that Saturday in May. I was a nine-year-old lad then and I can remember being with my dad at his mate's house and feeling pure excitement. There were other United fans there, as well as lads who were just on the beers, hoping for a Palace win so they could mock us supporters whose team had actually reached the final.

The two teams were led out by their respective managers, with Steve Coppell leading out Nigel Martyn, John Pemberton, Richard Shaw, Andy Gray, Gary O'Reilly, Andy Thorn, Phil Barber, Geoff Thomas, Mark Bright, John Salako and Alan Pardew. Ian Wright wasn't deemed fit enough after recovering from a broken leg suffered a few months earlier but was among the substitutes. Alex Ferguson proudly walked out in front of Jim Leighton, Paul Ince, Lee Martin, Steve Bruce, Mike Phelan, Gary Pallister, Bryan Robson, Neil Webb, Brian McClair, Mark Hughes and Danny Wallace. As the teams came out of the tunnel, there was an explosion of red and blue balloons from the Crystal Palace fans – the balloons were literally everywhere.

The teams lined up to meet the dignitaries, the stadium stood for the customary rendition of 'Abide With Me' and then it was showtime. United were in their all-white away kit while Palace wore their home strip of red and blue striped shirts, red shorts and red socks. The game started as you would expect from a cup final, with both sides feeling their way into the match, trying to find some rhythm. Liverpool had been undone by the set piece prowess of Palace in the semi-final, so it was no surprise when, in the 18th minute, the Eagles burst into the lead following a free kick on the right-hand touchline.

Phil Barber bent his cross in left-footed towards the edge of the six-yard box, where Gary O'Reilly outjumped his marker to nod into United's empty net. Jim Leighton had started to come for the cross but, at the last second, had decided to retreat, leaving him in no man's land. O'Reilly glanced his header towards goal and, with Leighton scrambling back towards his net and Steve Bruce coming back on to the line to try and hook the ball away, neither United player was able to clear the danger. 'And Crystal Palace take the lead, in precisely the way many people expected them to,' said BBC commentator John Motson. One half of Wembley Stadium were beside themselves, whereas the other half were stunned into silence. Much like the atmosphere at

Denzel's house. I was gutted but my dad said: 'Don't worry, son. Big pitch, big players, we will be fine.'

United came storming back and, in the 35th minute, the scores were level. And who else could have scored other than that man, Bryan Robson. The man for the big occasion had come up trumps yet again when United needed him the most. Just like my dad had said 15 minutes earlier. Big players always do the business. Paul Ince slipped the ball out to the right-hand side of the penalty area, from where Brian McClair played a low ball into the feet of Danny Wallace. Wallace's run pushed him away from goal, so the winger played the ball back to McClair and he delivered a first-time cross back into the mixer. Waiting at the back post, just six yards out, was Robson. It wasn't the best header you will ever see but, via a slight deflection from John Pemberton, United were level. It was 1-1 and that was the score as the teams went off for the half-time interval.

Following the break, both sides came out to play and United nearly took the lead when a long-range piledriver from Paul Ince was expertly tipped over the bar by Nigel Martyn. Then, just after the hour, Ferguson's team struck. It was a good goal in the way of a finish but it was so scrappy in how it came about. 'And I have to say that Palace's defence were pussyfooting around,' said Motson. A Palace defender had a chance to clear his line but Neil Webb threw himself in to block the ball and it ricocheted back behind the whole Palace defence, landing at the feet of Hughes. He lashed a left-footed strike past the helpless Martyn. I think the kids call it pressing nowadays.

Alex Ferguson jumped for joy on the Wembley bench, composed himself and immediately checked his watch to see how much time was remaining. There was loads. Ian Wright was brought on to replace Phil Barber in the 69th minute and the Eagles frontman made a devastating impact on the game. His first contribution was an explosive finish just three minutes after coming on. A ball from the midfield, played into the feet of Mark Bright, was turned around the corner first time and into the feet of Wright. The substitute, who had slipped into the left-hand channel, chopped back inside, leaving Pallister on his arse, before sliding the ball past Leighton and into the far bottom corner. Steve Coppell may have had an affinity towards United but he was out on the touchline in celebration of that goal and who could blame him?

Neither side could find a third goal and, as with both semi-finals, the teams were going to have to play an additional 30 minutes. Just as people were getting back from the toilets or the queues for refreshments, Palace took the lead. In the 92nd minute, a ball down towards the left flank was picked up by John Salako, who had Mike Phelan for company. Going nowhere, Salako checked back towards his own goal, looking like he was going to play the ball backwards, but somehow he managed to wrap his right foot around the ball. The cross evaded everyone, including a stranded Jim

Leighton and found its way to Ian Wright at the back post and he scored his second of the match. It wasn't just a brace for Wright that was a concern for United. Leighton had conceded three goals and for two of them, he was absolutely nowhere.

Now, Palace just had to cling on and FA Cup trophy would be in their hands for the first time in their history. But do you remember what my dad said about big players? With just seven minutes remaining, United launched a breakaway attack. Danny Wallace drove through the heart of the Eagles side and waited for Hughes to make his run behind the last defender before sliding him in. Hughes didn't even need to look at where the goal was, he just took the ball in his stride with a touch and fired the ball low and hard past Martyn. 'Hughes goes through the middle, chance here for 3-3 … Mark Hughes!' screeched John Motson. 'He's scored his second of the game and Manchester United have saved themselves.' It was just pure footballing theatre. And to think that this game had just continued in the same vein as the two semi-finals that preceded it. With neither team able to find a winner, they were going to have to do it all again in a replay on the Thursday night. Hopefully Steve Coppell had booked a hotel this time!

***

The replay threw a spanner in the works for England manager Bobby Robson, as the Three Lions had arranged two warm-up matches prior to Italia 90 and they fell either side of the replay. Bryan Robson was key to his namesake's World Cup plans but 'Captain Marvel' had a job to finish before he could link up with the national side. With England hosting Denmark at Wembley on Tuesday, 15 May, it meant the FA Cup replay had to be scheduled for the Thursday to allow 48 hours for the stadium to be cleaned and prepared.

British record signing Gary Pallister was sweating on his fitness ahead of the replay following a knock at the end of normal time on the Saturday. 'I twisted my ankle in the final minutes of normal time and had to come off early in extra time,' recalled Pallister in an interview with the *Daily Mail*. 'They actually scored during the final minutes I was on the pitch. Wrighty scored the third and the manager decided enough was enough. I was limping all around the pitch and so he took me off and put Mark Robins on. Then Sparky [Hughes] scored the third one. I'd gone off with my ankle injury and I'm sitting there praying we got the equaliser and earned the replay on the Thursday.'

Crystal Palace striker Ian Wright had set the final alight with his cameo appearance, scoring a brace on his return from a broken leg. Palace's marksman could have been forgiven for thinking that he had won the game for the south London outfit but Mark Hughes came up trumps to grab an equaliser when his team needed him the most. 'If I hadn't achieved anything else in my life, that memory would have been enough for me,' remembered Wright when looking back fondly on his cup final appearance. Wright twisted United centre-back Pallister inside out for his first and Palace's second goal, leaving him sprawling on the Wembley turf, and maybe that contributed to the injury problem which now threatened to rule him out of the replay.

It was going to go down to the wire for Ferguson's marquee transfer, with Pallister given until the final few hours before kick-off to prove his fitness, but that wasn't the only story on matchday that was about to make the headlines. 'I had ice on, I was getting more or less round-the-clock treatment from our physio Jim McGregor,' said Pallister. 'It was a race against time to be fit. I remember coming down to the team meeting the night before the game and it was still a little bit up in the air. I went into quite a solemn atmosphere and I was sat there and couldn't believe how down we were. There was a real hush in the room, there was no banter. I walked out with Brian McClair and I said "The lads seemed a bit down" and he said the gaffer had told the lads he'd dropped Jim Leighton at the start of the meeting. I'd missed that, I wasn't privy to that, so I'd gone through not knowing he'd been dropped. Jim was one of my neighbours, so obviously I was gutted for the guy. It was one hell of a brave call by the manager.'

In a final roll of the dice, Alex Ferguson had dropped the goalkeeper who had helped contribute to so much of the success during his time at Aberdeen before the manager eventually brought him down to Old Trafford. Personally, I thought Leighton had a torrid time that season but to drop him for the final replay was a ballsy move. Sealey, Ince, Pallister, Bruce, Martin, Phelan, Robson, Webb, McClair, Hughes and Wallace were dressed in their traditional kit of red shirts, white shorts and black socks as they again took to the field at Wembley. Palace were dressed in yellow and black stripes, black shorts and yellow socks. It was another full house under the twin towers and this time the match had to be completed on the night.

The nation had fallen in love with Crystal Palace's fairytale performances against Liverpool and in the first meeting with United but something had changed inside the Eagles dressing room in the lead-up to this encounter, with the team from south London ready for a war. They clattered and battered Les Sealey early on, clearly trying to upset his concentration, and the match began in a stop-start fashion due to all the niggly fouls that were being committed. It certainly wasn't the spectacle we had witnessed a few days earlier. 'I took a gamble replacing Jim Leighton,' admitted Ferguson. 'But I knew Les had the character and personality to play on the big stage.'

Crystal Palace tried to shake up the deputy stopper with, first, Mark Bright leaving one on him and then Andy Gray flattening Sealey, much to the annoyance of the United players. Sealey, however, was made of stern stuff. 'Palace players were trying to annoy me in the tunnel,' he said. 'Being a profound and deep-thinking person, I told them to fuck off! One of them called me an ugly bastard. "Less of the bastard" I said.' It was impossible not to love Les. His smile was infectious and his demeanour just rubbed off on the other players.

'Every day Les was here was like a birthday for him because he came out of nowhere to play in the cup final,' said team-mate Mike Phelan. 'He was always saying "I'm happy to be here" and the players took to him because of his attitude. Les was thrust straight into it but his off-the-cuff personality allowed him to adjust quite quickly. He could be relaxed or hyper, loud and funny or sometimes just a pain! With Les, what you saw was what you got.' And it was for this reason that Ferguson trusted his back-up keeper to play in what was, arguably, the biggest match of his tenure at the club to date.

If anyone who was lucky enough to grab a ticket for the second instalment of the 1990 FA Cup Final was thinking it was going to be anything like the first showing, then they were in for a long night. The first real event of note came after 20 minutes when Palace were awarded a free kick just yards outside Manchester United's penalty area. Nearly every man in red lined up in that wall, with the odd player flanking it, ready to charge down a quickly-taken effort. Screams of 'I can't see' echoed from Sealey as he attempted to line up his wall amongst a melee of bodies. Geoff Thomas stepped over the ball and Andy Gray rifled in a low effort that went through the wall and into the legs of the partially sighted Sealey.

That effort from Palace was the highlight of a turgid first 45 minutes in which both teams looked more scared to lose rather than attempting to try and win the match, but something had to give. Again, it was cagey from both teams in the early stages of the second half but in the 59th minute, United took the lead from an unlikely source. Paul Ince picked up the ball on the edge of United's penalty area before riding a tackle to start a counter-attack. He swiftly played the ball into the feet of McClair, who had started to make a move in the centre circle. Driving into the heart of the Palace midfield, McClair then played the ball out to the right-hand side, where Danny Wallace was patrolling the touchline. Wallace saw that there was nothing on ahead of him, so he played a ten-yard pass inside to the feet of Neil Webb. United's playmaker took one touch, looked up and saw the run of United's left-back Lee Martin out on the wing.

Webb played a beautiful 35-yard diagonal pass that Martin ran on to, taking the ball on his chest and, without even breaking stride, he let the ball bounce once before lashing it past Nigel Martyn who wouldn't have even seen it, such was the force of the shot. The ball flew into the roof of the net and one half of Wembley

Stadium erupted. 'Webb … Lee Martin, an inspired run from left-back on the far side. A chance here. And a goal!' shouted the ever-excitable John Motson on the BBC. 'What a tremendous run and Manchester United have taken the lead and Lee Martin, made a run from left-back that was 40/50 yards, took it on his chest and smashed it with his right foot past Martyn and, with an hour gone, Manchester United have taken the lead because Andy Gray couldn't get to him.'

While the goalscorer was flattened by his team-mates during the celebrations, Crystal Palace had to pick themselves up and go again. They had twice come back against Liverpool and again against United in the first tie, but this was going to be one mountain too many for the Eagles, as they looked to have had the wind knocked out of their sails. Steve Coppell's side tried to throw everything at Alex Ferguson's men but United defended like their lives depended on it. Sealey was coming for every cross and taking an absolute age to clear his lines. After referee Allan Gunn looked at his watch for the umpteenth time, he finally blew his whistle and ended what was a mammoth cup final over 180 enthralling minutes.

The players rushed over to congratulate the manager, who had been taking bullets for them all season, as well as their deputy goalkeeper, who had come through the barrage of dirty tactics from Palace to ensure that United kept a clean sheet and lift the club's seventh FA Cup.

Coppell shook the hands of his opposite number as his team climbed the Wembley steps to collect their runners-up medals. Then it was the turn of those beautiful boys in red. I can remember sitting and watching, trying to take it all in, as Bryan Robson led the team up those 39 steps towards the royal Box. Shaking the hands of the dignitaries, 'Captain Marvel' made his way along the line before he was presented with the cup. It was swathed in red, white and black ribbons. Robson took his medal, grabbed the cup and turned to lift it high above his head just as he had done previously in 1983 and 1985.

It must have felt like a release valve for the manager following the tirade of abuse he had received over the course of that season. 'Without the FA Cup victory over Crystal Palace nearly four years after my arrival, grave doubts would have been raised about my suitability for the job,' Ferguson wrote in his autobiography. 'We will never know how close I was to being sacked, because the decision was never forced on the United board. But without that triumph at Wembley, the crowds would have shrivelled. Disaffection might have swept the club. Winning the 1990 FA Cup allowed us breathing space and deepened my sense that this was a wonderful club with which to win trophies. To win the FA Cup at Wembley made the good times roll. But on the morning after our victory, one newspaper declared "Okay, you've proved you can win the FA Cup, now go back to Scotland". I never forgot that.'

Gary Pallister had made it through the match despite his injury scare and remembers the events of the night like they were yesterday. 'I've seen the replay of the game not so long ago,' recalls Pallister. 'Crystal Palace seemed obsessed with trying to unsettle Les Sealey, who came in for Jim, and a few hefty challenges went on in the early part of the game to try and knock the confidence out of him. They tried to play on his big-match nerves but Les was a confident character and he produced a couple of great saves to help us win the game that night. Around the hour mark, I remember seeing Lee Martin pop up in the left-wing position and smash it into the roof of the net.

'The funniest thing was that for the next minute and a half, he was in a daydream. They kicked off and attacked down the right-hand side and he was somewhere else. He'd probably seen the headlines about him. He eventually managed to get back on track and we saw the game out. It wasn't as exciting as the game on the Saturday but it was important for the club to get a win and it was the start of the confidence building in the club and the start of big things.'

While for some, it was a time of euphoric delight, spare a thought for the man who had been left out of the replay at the very last minute and if you want to know just what type of character his deputy was, well then look no further than here. Les Sealey found Jim Leighton crying after the match and tried to console him before giving him his winner's medal. Leighton refused to accept it but Sealey wouldn't take no for an answer. Then, when Les wasn't looking, Leighton slipped the medal inside Sealey's blazer pocket. On finding the medal later on, Sealey handed it to Bobby Charlton with strict instructions to make sure it reached Leighton. Later that summer, Ferguson returned for Sealey and offered him a one-year deal, as well as handing him back the medal that Leighton had point blank refused to accept. It now sits proudly on display in the museum at Old Trafford. When Les Sealey passed away in 2001, Leighton carried the coffin for the man who had replaced him, such was the respect between the two goalkeepers.

A few years after the final, Leighton spoke out over being left out of the replay, insisting that he would never forgive the man who made the decision that day. 'We've never spoken since and never will do again,' insisted Leighton when quizzed about his relationship with Ferguson. 'I had been fortunate enough to win quite a few medals up to that time and, unless I could walk up the stairs and wear the hat and the scarf and lift the cup, then I didn't want anybody's charity.' It was a decision that hadn't been taken lightly by the boss but one that ultimately paid off. 'It was an animal instinct. I had to discard poor old Jim,' Ferguson said in the aftermath. 'My conscience is clear. I have never done anything like it before and I don't want to do anything like it again – ever.'

Despite the story surrounding Leighton, the players headed back to their hotel for the biggest party of the season. 'We had a big do with the families,' said Pallister. 'The manager always said "If you win something, you celebrate it well" and we certainly did that night. We did the bus tour around Manchester. It gave you a taste for winning things and enjoying it. That was the catalyst.' There was one noticeable absentee from the bash. Les Sealey had decided to head back to east London, grabbing a lift back from a photographer, because he had promised someone that he would be at a pub quiz. On his way around the North Circular road, he unwound his window and began shouting at groups of Manchester United supporters making their way into the London night.

'What's happening? What cup? Who was the goalkeeper? How did he play? Did he really make a difference? What's his name? Did he have one of these?', at which point Sealey was waving his goalkeeping shirt out of the car window. One supporter shouted back 'It fucking well is you, isn't it.' The fans were clearly confused, given that Sealey should have been sipping champagne in a swanky London hotel but was instead stuck in traffic in a clapped-out old Sierra. But that was Les. He was just different. God rest his soul.

For the goalscoring hero of the day, it could have been so different. Talking to *Goal,* Lee Martin recalled how a misunderstanding led to him scoring the winner. 'I was trying to run out the way,' Martin joked. 'I was about 20 yards from the bench and I heard assistant manager Archie Knox shout for me to get forward. I was in my own box and he shouted at me, so I made a run of 70 or 80 yards to the edge of the box. Neil Webb played a great ball and, as I chested it, I was just about to pull my leg back to strike it and I got cramp in my calf. I thought "Just hit it". I managed to get my foot on it and it flew in the top corner. I realised I had scored but my leg locked up with cramp and I was in absolute agony.'

With Martin laid out on the turf, his team-mates bundled him to offer their congratulations but United's left-back was in a bit of a daze. 'As I got up, Robbo was slapping my face asking if I was all right. He told me I'd be fine and I made it through to the final whistle. It was just amazing. Not a chance did I think when I woke up on the morning of the game that I would score. That scenario just never entered my mind. As a kid, you dream about scoring the winning goal in a cup final but, with my record as a goalscorer in the first team, it just didn't add up. I was 60/1 to score, I think. Some of my mates had put a tenner on it, so won £600, which was a lot of money back then. In the dressing room after the game, Archie came and sat next to me and said he wasn't actually shouting at me to get forward – he was shouting at someone else. So, it shouldn't have been me that scored that goal!'

Much was said about the difference between the two teams competing in that final, given that United's squad had cost more than £12m to assemble. Yet, it was a player from the youth ranks, who cost absolutely nothing, who scored the goal and a goalkeeper on loan who kept a clean sheet as United won a trophy and, in effect, keep the manager in his job. If you have never seen the film *Sliding Doors,* then I urge you to watch it to fully understand the 'what ifs' and 'what might have beens' that run throughout the course of this 1989/90 season. What if Mark Robins hadn't have scored at Forest or Hereford United had sprung a surprise? Or maybe Micky Quinn and Mark McGhee could have run riot on Tyneside. What if Dave Bassett had worked his magic in Sheffield or Joe Royle's plucky Oldham or Steve Coppell's Palace had managed to take the spoils? But they didn't.

Lee Martin's season had, in fact, gone full circle. If you go back to the Nottingham Forest win in the third round, Mark Robins was rightly given the plaudits and is often cited as the reason for Ferguson keeping his job but, if you take a closer look at the build-up to that goal, Martin just about managed to keep the ball in play on the left touchline and, if he had failed to do so, it would have resulted in a Nottingham Forest throw-in. Instead, Martin kept the ball alive before playing a pass inside to Mark Hughes, who caressed the ball into the path of the goalscorer Robins. Fast forward to May and Martin finished the move that ultimately won the cup for the Red Devils.

Another trophy had found its way into the Old Trafford trophy cabinet, like many had done before.

Lee Martin and the 60/1 Shot

LEE ANDREW Martin came through the youth set-up at Manchester United before eventually making his first-team debut at the tail end of the 1987/88 campaign, coming on as a substitute in a 2-1 win over Wimbledon at Old Trafford on 9 May 1988. The Red Devils had finished runners-up to Liverpool, who had ended the season with a nine-point cushion over Ferguson's men, the closest the club had been to a title tilt since Dave Sexton's second-place finish in 1978/79. So near and yet so far, but it was now a chance for Martin to lay a claim for the left-back position in the team. Arthur Albiston had moved to West Bromwich Albion to link up with former boss Ron Atkinson and Colin Gibson had been cursed with injuries during his time at the club.

The following season would see Martin appear on a regular basis, scoring his first goal for the club in January 1989 in a 3-1 win at West Ham United. Comfortable with both feet, Martin could slot into either full-back position – something Denis Irwin was later able to do for

Ferguson when he signed the right-back from Oldham Athletic following those two blockbuster semi-final matches, eventually moving the right-footed Irwin to left-back. Martin's versatility meant that he featured in the majority of league and cup games during the 1989/90 campaign, culminating in his leading role in the Wembley showpiece as the curtain came down on what was a rollercoaster of a season.

On the *UTD Podcast*, Martin recalled both Wembley meetings with Palace. 'The Saturday game was 3-3 and it was a brilliant game,' he said. 'I remember Mark Hughes saying to me in the warm-up "Make sure you enjoy this experience because you might never come back again". They were brilliant words.' Martin also revealed he might not have started the final replay had he told the manager the truth about his fitness in training. 'I had a bit of problems with cramp, every game, even the league games, the last five-six minutes. I remember training in London on the Wednesday, the manager pulled me to one side and said "Are you going to be all right tomorrow with your cramp and all that?" and I went "Yeah, absolutely fine, no problem whatsoever". I was never going to say no. It was a cup final. It was probably a daft question. I said "I'll be fine, don't worry".'

A lot was said at the time about the odds of Martin actually finding the net prior to kick-off. 'I think I was 60/1 to score. The goalkeepers were only 50/1. They gave me no chance,' he told *UTD Podcast,* before describing the moment that wrote his name into United folklore. 'Mark Hughes had made a run across the box to take a couple of defenders away and Neil Webb probably played the best ball he ever played, right into my chest on the edge of the box. I chested it down and just as I was about to hit it, I got cramp in my calf, so I thought "Jesus". This is only in a split second. I could feel the cramp coming on but I thought "I've just got to get a foot on the ball", so I managed to stretch my foot out, got a foot on the ball and it flew into the top corner. You wouldn't believe it. It was so lucky. Normally, it would have gone into the stands somewhere but it flew in and I thought "Jesus, it's gone in, that!"'

Despite being susceptible to cramping up, Martin managed to see out the remainder of the match and rejoiced at the final whistle with his manager and team-mates. 'When the final whistle went, all the lads came running on the pitch,' the former full-back remembers. 'The manager put his arm around us, saying "Well done". The manager, with his watch and his phone, was then thrown in the bath. It was just brilliant. It was a brilliant occasion.'

* * *

Lee Martin very kindly shared his memories of that time with me. Back in 1990, I was a nine-year-old lad wearing the full kit and watching events unfold on the TV, wondering if this was how every cup final played out. I've since found out that this isn't the case but that feeling of watching those two final games will live with me for the rest of my life.

That goal was 35 years ago now Lee, does it make you feel old? Yes, feeling old now but it's nice people still remember the game 35 years on.

You had been playing left-back for large periods of that season and even the season before. Was it a position you enjoyed or was it a case of now you're in the team you just got your head down and got on with it to do a job for the manager? No, I really enjoyed playing left-back. I was comfortable with both feet and the manager encouraged his full-backs to get forward and join in with the play.

Could you feel at that time that there was noise outside of the dressing room in terms of the team having to finally win the league again? I know it had been a long time but the manager kept us in the moment and concentrated on each game. Having supported the club since the age of seven, I knew that we were always under pressure to win trophies.

Were the players aware of the building pressure around the manager at the time or was it just business as usual? I think at the time we could see what the manager was building and knew the board had faith in him and, as a young lad, I was just enjoying playing for Manchester United and if we won something, then it was a bonus.

Sounds like you were living every Manchester United fan's dream, Lee. The win at Nottingham Forest

seemed to build momentum. You managed to keep the ball in, just inside the left-hand touchline, which led to the build-up and eventual goal. Some ball from Sparky as well, wasn't it? Outside of the boot and on to the head of Mark Robins, who stooped down to head home. Yes, they were attacking down their right-hand side and I won the ball and kept it in play, giving it to Hughes, who put a great ball in. Mark Robins was probably the best finisher in the box, so I knew he could finish it. I'd carried on my run into the box and if the goalkeeper had parried ball out, I was there to finish it but luckily Mark put it in the net.

The games were coming thick and fast then. How did the manager keep you all focused, with the team sitting in a precarious position in the table? The manager was brilliant at preparing the team for matchdays. The training was fun during the week but we knew when matchday came around, we had to be ready and focused to win the games and push ourselves up the table. We also had a great leader in Bryan Robson when we were out there on the pitch.

Some player was 'Captain Marvel'.

Did it bother any of the lads that you were drawn away from home each round? No, that didn't bother us at all. We had some good draws and managed to get to Wembley. I'm not sure if it has been done since. **Unfortunately, Lee, Manchester City equalled the feat in the 2018/19 season.**

You picked up a knock in that fascinating 3-3 draw in the first final. Were you ever concerned that you could

miss the replay? I had a bit of cramp at the end of the 3-3. It had been a long season up 'til then but I knew I'd be okay for the replay the following Thursday.

Scoring that goal and then winning the match must have been amazing. How good was that feeling when you walked up those famous steps to get the trophy and receive your medal? It was what I'd dreamt about since I was seven, so it was very special. The best moment of the whole experience was walking out of the tunnel at Wembley on the Saturday. It was a nice sunny day, with a capacity crowd of 80,000 people, but scoring the winner was pretty good too.

Lee, may you dine out on that goal for the rest of your days.

Epilogue – Out of the Darkness, Comes Light

HAVING LIFTED the FA Cup, United were then entered into the European Cup Winners' Cup for the following campaign. It was the first season that English clubs, other than Liverpool, were allowed back into European competition following the Heysel disaster and a blanket ban for our clubs, which lasted five seasons. There were trips to Pécsi Munkás, Wrexham, Montpellier, Legia Warsaw and then Rotterdam, where United would face Johan Cruyff's Barcelona in the final. A 2-1 victory brought more silverware, this time on a larger stage. A sixth-place finish in the league had shown that the club was on an upward trajectory, despite losing to Second Division Sheffield Wednesday in the League Cup Final.

The following season – the last for the old First Division before the launch of the Premier League – saw United go toe to toe with Leeds United, only for the club from over the Pennines to nick it at the final furlong and deny the Red Devils a long-awaited title. Even with the despair of not winning the league, there was still more silverware added. The European Super Cup and the League Cup (the club's first) were hoisted aloft that season but the fans were again yearning for the big fish in the shape of the First Division title.

The 1992/93 season saw the birth of the Premier League and what can only be described as the coming of age of this United team under Ferguson. While the cups had continued to roll into the Old Trafford trophy room, focus switched to the title. French forward Eric Cantona had just helped Leeds United to the title but he swapped white rose for red and hotfooted it across to Lancashire in a transfer that no one saw coming. It would provide the catalyst for a title charge and this time the team did get over the line.

It wasn't without its dramas, though. With just six games to go and United trailing at home to Sheffield Wednesday, Steve Bruce headed two goals, including one deep into stoppage time, to turn the game on its head and give United the momentum to go on and lift the trophy at the expense of Aston Villa. The phrase 'Fergie time' was born. 'That night, I watched the video of the second half and used my stopwatch to time all the stoppages for injuries and substitutions,' wrote Sir Alex in his autobiography. 'There should, in fact, have been an additional 12 minutes.' Finally, 26 seasons after the last title, United were the kings of England once more. 'I'm proud of the players and really pleased for the chairman, the supporters and everyone connected with the club,' said Ferguson. 'Some of the people concerned have been connected with the club for all those 26 years and it's fantastic for them.'

Cantona and Co. continued in the same vein the following season, this time adding a first league and FA Cup Double to the club's honours list. A 4-0 victory at Wembley over the season's bogey team, Chelsea, put a beautiful cherry on an already fantastic cake. The Blues had edged out United 0-1 on both occasions in the league but this time out, the Red Devils provided the biggest winning margin in an FA Cup Final. Ferguson knew prior to kick-off that United would be in devastating form that day. 'All week he went on,' said Steve Bruce, reflecting on that soaking wet day under the twin towers. 'The manager said if we score first against Chelsea, we will win four- or five-nil. It's the FA Cup Final, you don't win FA Cup Finals by four or five, not very often anyway.'

Bruce was intrigued by his manager's confidence. 'I remember asking him when we were walking off the training ground "Boss, can I ask you, where do you get that from?" He goes "Because Glenn Hoddle is substitute, he's not got the legs anymore, especially at Wembley, and he'll bring himself on in sacrifice of his defensive set-up. And he'll come on in the middle of the pitch and he can't run anymore and we'll swamp through the middle." And that was exactly how that day unfolded. In fact, if you go back through the footage, as Cantona tucks away his second penalty on 67 minutes, the camera pans to Hoddle who, as predicted, is unzipping his tracksuit top to enter the fray.

Winning the Double was a fantastic achievement and, at this point, the MUFC train was really gaining momentum. Only a 3-1 defeat at Wembley to Aston Villa in the League Cup Final halted what would have been a domestic Treble. It was at this point that opponents in the Premier League were really struggling to deal with the football that was being played by Ferguson's men. The club were looking for a hat-trick of domestic titles in 1995 but when Eric Cantona was banned for assaulting a Crystal Palace supporter, United's defence of their trophies was derailed. First, there was the cruel final-day draw at West Ham United that handed Blackburn Rovers the title and then a 1-0 defeat to Everton in the FA Cup Final meant that, for the first time in five years, Ferguson and his United team would have nothing to show for their efforts.

Cantona's ban ran until 1 October 1995, the player returning just in time to jumpstart the team's title charge that season. The enigmatic Frenchman scored on his return against rivals Liverpool in a 2-2 draw and, over the remainder of that campaign, scored a raft of vital goals to help United secure another title, their third in four seasons. There was also another FA Cup Final, their fourth in seven seasons, and it was the team Eric had made his comeback against, Liverpool, who provided the opposition. Who else would score the winner in a 1-0 victory but Eric Cantona. His goal epitomised his importance to the team that season and how much they had missed him a year earlier.

A fourth title in five years followed in 1997 but possibly the most cataclysmic news that dropped at the tail end of that campaign was not the euphoria of claiming another Premier League title but Cantona's announcement that he was retiring from football with immediate effect. Now, footballers retire all the time but not at the age of 30 when at the peak of their footballing powers. But that was Eric. Breezed in, did the business and left in the blink of an eye.

There was now a huge void in the United team but Ferguson moved swiftly to try and plug the gap left by Cantona with the signing of Teddy Sheringham from Tottenham Hotspur. Arsenal would begin their golden period under Arsene Wenger in 1998 and won both the Premier League and the FA Cup, leaving the Red Devils to lick their wounds. Injuries to key players for prolonged periods of time meant that, by the time the title race reached its climax, United had been unable to keep their powder dry and Arsenal roared past them over the finish line. Suddenly, the loss of Cantona was magnified, such was the lack of firepower when the season drew into the finale, a time when you need that extra bit of magic to unlock defences.

Ferguson could sense there was a change needed and made two major signings the following summer, bringing in Jaap Stam and Dwight Yorke from PSV Eindhoven and Aston Villa, respectively. Roy Keane had returned from a year's absence but, as the festive period began, United were stuttering in sixth place. Once the calendar changed to 1999, so did something inside that dressing room. United would not lose another game in any competition, claiming an historic Treble of Premier League (it was won on the final day), the FA Cup (a 2-0 defeat of Newcastle United) and the Champions League when a crazy final three minutes in Barcelona saw Ferguson and his charges reach the promised land by beating Bayern Munich 2-1.

While dominating the Premier League since the early 1990s, Alex Ferguson had become hamstrung on the European stage due to the three-foreigner rule that was in place. For most of the sides on the continent, 95 per cent of their playing quota were homegrown players, so the ruling didn't have such a debilitating effect, but English clubs had, for decades, filled their squads with players from Scotland, Wales, Northern Ireland and the Republic of Ireland. All these players were considered to fall under the rule. On one occasion when United faced Barcelona at the Camp Nou, the rule forced Ferugson to play a makeshift side and the result was a 4-0 humbling.

Although the rule was eventually scrapped during the 1995/96 season, Ferguson said: 'It's come two years too late for us because we'd have had a chance of winning the European Cup in 1994 otherwise.' It was no coincidence that the following season United reached the semi-finals of the Champions League, only to lose to eventual winners Borussia Dortmund. Just two years later, the zenith of European football was reached. The boss had done his homework on opponents Bayern and his work came up trumps.

'It's easy to say this but the homework won us the game,' he later told Ally McCoist on TNT Sports. 'In the analysis of Bayern, in big games particularly, they used to take the two wide players off and go into a tight midfield. Having no Roy Keane and Paul Scholes, I had to gamble on my midfield. I wanted to make sure we had passing ability and decided to put David Beckham in midfield alongside Nicky Butt. Nicky did all sorts of jobs and Giggsy [Ryan Giggs] wide right and [Jesper] Blomqvist wide left. Didn't work in the first half, at all. I was waiting for them to make the substitution. The minute he made the substitution, I went three in the middle and three up.

'I brought on Teddy Sheringham. I said "Teddy, you go and play up top on the right centre-back, try and pull the right-back in". With Giggs playing in the left of midfield, it was really suited to him. Because running off the space all the time, Beckham, on the right-hand side, started to get crosses in. In the last 15 minutes, we made a lot of chances. Having said that, we could have been out long before that. They hit the crossbar, missed a couple of chances, Peter Schmeichel made a couple of saves. It was amazing.'

Having led the team to an unprecedented Treble, Ferguson was knighted in the 1999 New Year's Honours list for his services to football and the remarkable never say die attitude he had instilled in his teams over the last decade. The boss said he was 'delighted and honoured' to receive such a prestigious avward and follow in the footsteps of another Manchester United manager, Sir Matt Busby.

The following two seasons saw Sir Alex remain at the top of English football, with Manchester United retaining the title in both 2000 and 2001. It looked like there was going to be a fourth title in a row in 2002 but Arsenal, who had been clinging on like a heavyweight boxer hoping for a points decision, finally broke through the Manchester stranglehold. It was only the third season in 12 years that the fruits of their labour had yielded nothing. Sir Alex had planned to retire at the end of the campaign but a change of heart over the Christmas period heralded an upturn in United's form, although it wasn't enough.

With Sir Alex now back in full flow, an assault on the Premier League was on the agenda once more. Ruud Van Nistelrooy had been brought in a year earlier to provide the firepower and had hit a barnstorming number of goals in his maiden season. This time, however, they counted for something, as United were the cream of the crop again in 2003. It did signal the end of David Beckham's time in Manchester, with a move to Real Madrid that summer following a strained relationship with the boss.

The team were starting to evolve as the old guard of the Treble-winning season began to head out of the door to be replaced by a new, younger generation. Cristiano Ronaldo had been brought in from Sporting Lisbon to inject a little bit of young magic into the squad but, with the transition of the squad coming at the same time that Arsenal were reaching the peak of their powers under Wenger, another title tilt was too far out of reach for Sir Alex and the boys. Instead, they had to sit back and watch the Gunners go a whole season unbeaten, clinching the Premier League title without tasting defeat. The FA Cup was clinched in Cardiff with a 3-0 win over Millwall and, although this was a welcome trophy at the end of the season, it was the league title the manager wanted to win back.

It was a feeling that was going to be extended over the next two seasons. Jose Mourinho walked into Chelsea in 2004, having just won the Champions League with Porto, and was handed the keys to Stamford Bridge and a blank cheque book. Mourinho's Chelsea steamrollered the Premier League for two seasons running while Ferguson was still trying to put together the pieces of the puzzle at Old Trafford. Three years seemed an eternity for Ferguson, who had a near monopoly on the league for the previous 15 seasons. Wayne Rooney had been signed from Everton, a talented youngster, to provide the firepower to get back on top.

In the summer of 2006, the missing parts of the machine seemed to slot in seamlessly. Michael Carrick was signed from Tottenham Hotspur and instantly struck up a partnership with Paul Scholes in the centre of midfield. The team seemed to click back into gear and they eventually overhauled Chelsea to reclaim the title after a barren three-year spell. Henrik Larsson had joined on loan during the winter months and the move proved to be a masterstroke. Cristiano Ronaldo had suddenly become a goalscoring machine and his great partnership with Rooney, which saw the pair score 46 goals between them, was the driving force towards the title. United were only extra time away from a domestic Double before Mourinho had the last laugh as United fell 1-0 to Chelsea in the FA Cup Final.

The following campaign saw an interesting signing in Carlos Tevez on loan from West Ham. Tevez linked up brilliantly with Ronaldo and Rooney, who was now banging in goals for fun, helping the club to another championship. Ronaldo found the net on 40 occasions, alerting the attention of Real Madrid, a club he had supported as a boy. United also found form in the Champions League and when they dispatched Barcelona in the semi-finals, it lined up an all-English final with

Chelsea. Mourinho had been relieved of his duties prior to the Blues' run to Moscow but, even so, this was a Mourinho team that faced United in that final.

It was a tight and tense affair, as all finals are, with Ronaldo heading United into the lead with his 41st goal of the season before Frank Lampard equalised just before half-time to send the teams in level. United lived a charmed life in the second period, with Chelsea banging on the door but unable to find a way through. The game petered out into a 1-1 draw and the lottery of penalties. When Nicolas Anelka had his spot kick saved by Edwin van der Sar, United players were left celebrating in the Manchester-style rain in Moscow. It was an impressive league and European Double. 'I feel proud, very, very proud,' Sir Alex said. 'Sometimes you have to pinch yourself but we won't get carried away with it. Tomorrow, I'll be thinking of next season. It drains away quickly for me. The euphoria evaporates almost immediately. The moment of that final penalty save from Edwin van der Sar, that was my moment, my euphoria and excitement, then you just carry on.'

Attention from the Spanish capital on Ronaldo grew to the point where it looked like he would not be coming back for another season at Old Trafford. Speaking to *The Guardian,* the forward said: 'I can confirm that I'll be playing for Manchester United next season. I'll be playing with my heart and soul and I will fight and honour the shirt with the same desire and dedication as

I always have. My coach [Ferguson] was kind enough to come and see me in Lisbon a few days ago. It was a very honest conversation between two people that respect each other and that, I'm sure, share a mutual affection and friendship. Sir Alex listened to me, I listened to him and we established that the best for both sides would be for me to continue at Old Trafford. It's no sacrifice for me, it's a great honour. I have important things to win in England. I want to defend the European title and help United become world champions, not forgetting the Premier League and other competitions.'

The 2008/09 season saw the team kick on again, claiming another domestic Double. This time, however, it was in the shape of the Premier League, the team's third in a row, and the League Cup, following a penalty shoot-out victory over Tottenham Hotspur after a 0-0 stalemate at Wembley. Dimitar Berbatov had been signed from Spurs in the summer and chipped in with 14 goals in his maiden campaign. Ferguson's men claimed the World Club Cup and reached a second consecutive Champions League Final in Rome, where, in Pep Guardiola's Barcelona, they faced arguably one of the greatest club sides to have ever played the game.

Even with Ronaldo at his peak, having scored 26 goals that season, United didn't have enough to cope with the Catalan giants. Barca won the European showpiece 2-0 and United barely laid a glove on their opponents. 'We didn't play as well as we can but you have to give Barcelona credit,' said the United manager. 'Lionel Messi wasn't the problem. Xavi and Andres Iniesta kept the ball all night and made it difficult for us. The disappointment was the use of the ball when we got possession. You have to wait minutes to get it back off them. Could be it was an off night. Could be it was a mountain too big to climb. The better team won and there's nothing we can do about that now.'

Despite Ronaldo having insisted a year earlier that he had a desire to stay in Manchester, United were powerless to stop him moving to Madrid that summer. Another big player had left the club but we had been here before many times. Nothing lasts forever in life or in sport – the wheel turns, the clock ticks on and change happens as surely as night follows day. Michael Owen was signed from Newcastle United to add more depth to the striking options, with the forward now approaching the twilight of his career. It was still a shrewd move by the manager, who was now facing scrutiny in the market following the record-breaking fee received for Ronaldo.

The new season looked likely to yield a record fourth successive top-flight title when Wayne Rooney broke the 30-goal barrier by Easter, only for the striker to pick up an injury that ruled him out for the rest of the season. With the goals starting to dry up, Chelsea pipped United at the death, including a controversial win at Old Trafford following an offside decision that had Ferguson spitting feathers. 'That's twice we've been beaten by refereeing decisions. It happened at Stamford Bridge as well,' Ferguson said. 'The linesman is right in front of Drogba and he gets it wrong. It was a poor, poor performance from the officials in a game of this magnitude.'

Again, the League Cup was reclaimed following a 2-1 victory over Aston Villa, with Owen netting for the Red Devils, but it was the manner in which the team had given up the title that stung Ferguson. Dimitar Berbatov was left with the task of firing the team towards glory in the absence of Rooney but it was a tall order and one that the Bulgarian fell just short of. The manager claimed that the team were looking 'leggy' with the number of matches played over the last couple of seasons but it was a double-edged sword. More games played mean you are being successful.

What had become a habit for Ferguson was that for every title that had been missed, the team found a way to regain it as quickly as possible. Since the first Premier League win back in 1993, the club's longest streak without tasting title champagne was the three years between 2003 and 2006. Again, the team dusted themselves down and Rooney was back and firing, forging a strike partnership with Berbatov that helped the Bulgarian to more than 20 goals. The team had certainly missed the spark and creativity of Rooney in the dying embers of the previous season, such was his importance.

Another striker had also been added into the mix, a little Mexican by the name of Javier Hernández. The 'Little Pea' made an instant impact, scoring on his debut in the Community Shield win against Chelsea and his involvement during the course of the season was invaluable for the team as the forward trio dovetailed together perfectly like Rooney, Ronaldo and Tevez had done before them. United had to wait until February to face their first defeat of the season. Hernández's most important contribution was arguably his and United's opening goal against the Blues at Old Trafford that all but sealed the deal as United reclaimed the Premier League title at the expense of rivals Chelsea.

What was the most significant aspect of this championship was that it had taken United ahead of rivals Liverpool in terms of league titles. United now sat on 19 while those down the East Lancs Road held 18. Ferguson had been taking quite a few sly comments from former Liverpool players, mainly Alan Hansen, who had a regular newspaper column and had openly questioned Ferguson on multiple occasions, most notably with his comments on *Match of the Day* in 1995. 'The trick is always buy when you're strong, so he needs to buy players. You can't win anything with kids,' said Hansen, to which the team responded with a league and cup double in 1996. This time, Hansen questioned whether Ferguson still had the same desire to win following back-to-back defeats. The boss responded: 'My greatest challenge is not what's happening at the moment, my greatest challenge was knocking Liverpool right off their fucking perch. And you can print that.'

Across the way, Manchester City were taken over in 2008 by Sheikh Mansour of the Abu Dhabi royal family and were making the most of their new-found wealth, including taking Carlos Tevez across the divide. Much to the annoyance of the manager, a giant advertising board was unveiled in the city bearing the slogan 'Welcome to Manchester' and featuring Tevez's image in a shade of sky blue. 'At the moment, we have a neighbour and, sometimes, the neighbours are noisy,' said Ferguson. 'You can't do anything about them, you gotta go on with your life.'

Unfortunately for United, those neighbours had become the driving force by the 2011/12 season, taking Ferguson and his men right to the wire. In fact, it went deep into injury time of the final match of the season. United had already beaten Sunderland 1-0 at the Stadium of Light to have one hand on the Premier League title but Manchester City were still playing at home to Queens Park Rangers. QPR led 2-1 with just seconds remaining before Edin Džeko equalised in the 92nd minute to give City a glimmer of hope. Then, with literally the last kick of the season, Sergio Aguero broke United hearts with a 94th-minute strike that handed City the title.

Ferguson had won the championship three times on the final day so had nothing but respect for his City counterparts. 'It is a cruel way to have the title ripped away but I've had a lot of ups and downs in my 25 years here,' he said. 'Today, we nearly did it and I would like to say on behalf of Manchester United, congratulations to our neighbours. It's a fantastic achievement. This is not an easy league – it's the hardest league in the world – and anybody that wins it deserves it.' Patrice Evra recalled the words the boss told the players in the dressing room after the news had filtered through. 'When we lost on that final day, people were crying. Ferguson told us to feel it, to hurt. I did an interview and said we would win it back by ten points next season – we won it by 13.'

Ferguson's first task in his quest to regain the title was to prize Robin van Persie away from rivals Arsenal in what some considered a major coup and the Dutchman wasted no time in introducing himself to the Stretford End with a flurry of goals in the infancy of his United career. Rooney again, like a striking chameleon, such was his skill of striking up an instant link with his new team-mates, helped Van Persie to 30 goals and the team to another Premier League title, Ferguson's 13th, and the club's 20th top-flight success. As the team headed towards the title, Ferguson broke the news that he was set to retire at the end of the season. 'It is the right time,' he said. 'It was important to me to leave the organisation in the best possible shape and I believe I have done so.'

His players lined up on either side of the tunnel to form a guard of honour. Their manager was set to take to the Old Trafford pitch for one final time. Ferguson had announced his retirement a few months previously and this time he meant it. His initial date was set back in 2001. Fortunately for the club and Manchester United fans all over the world, Ferguson was talked out of it by his family. This time around, though, the decision was final.

The crowning glory of that long, last walk from changing room to centre circle was that United had clinched yet another Premier League title. The boss brought down the curtain on the 2012/13 season and his 26-year stint at Old Trafford by addressing the crowd.

Ferguson took the microphone and said: 'I've got no script in my mind. I'm just going to ramble on and hope I get to the core of what this club is meant to be. First of all, it's a thank you to Manchester United; not just the directors, not just the medical staff, the coaching staff, the players, the supporters – it's all of you. You have been the most fantastic experience of my life. Thank you.'

He continued: 'I have been very fortunate. I have been able to manage some of the greatest players in the country, let alone Manchester United. All these players here today have represented our club in the proper way. They have won a championship in a fantastic fashion. Well done to the players. My retirement doesn't mean the end of my life with the club. I will now be able to enjoy watching them rather than suffer with them. If you think about it, those last-minute goals, the comebacks – even the defeats – are all part of this great football club of ours. It has been an unbelievable experience for all of us, so thank you for that. I'd also like to remind you that when we had bad times here, the club stood by me, all my staff stood by me, the players stood by me. Your job now is to stand by our new manager. That is important.'

During Sir Alex's final season, Harvard Business School professor Anita Elberse had the unique opportunity to observe Ferguson's management style in a series of visits and in-depth interviews. Anita drove into the core of what Ferguson believed in when he walked through those doors at Old Trafford in the autumn of 1986. Below is an extract from the *Harvard Business Review* in which Elberse probed the boss.

'From the moment I got to Manchester United, I thought of only one thing: building a football club. I wanted to build right from the bottom. That was in order to create fluency and a continuity of supply to the first team. With this approach, the players all grow up together, producing a bond that, in turn, creates a spirit.

'When I arrived, only one player on the first team was under 24. Can you imagine that, for a club like Manchester United? I knew that a focus on youth would fit the club's history and my earlier coaching experience told me that winning with young players could be done and that I was good at working with them. So, I had the confidence and conviction that if United was going to mean anything again, rebuilding the youth structure was crucial. You could say it was brave but fortune favours the brave.

'The first thought of 99 per cent of newly appointed managers is to make sure they win – to survive. So, they bring experienced players in. That's simply because we're in a results-driven industry. At some clubs, you need only to lose three games in a row and you're fired. In today's football world, with a new breed of directors and owners, I am not sure any club would have the patience to wait for a manager to build a team over a four-year period.

'Winning a game is only a short-term gain – you can lose the next game. Building a club brings stability and consistency. You don't ever want to take your eyes off the first team but our youth development efforts ended up leading to our many successes in the 1990s and early 2000s. The young players really became the spirit of the club.'

In a 26-year span at the club, ironically the same amount of time United went without lifting the championship, Sir Alex won the following honours:

Premier League 1992/93, 1993/94, 1995/96, 1996/97, 1998/99, 1999/2000, 2000/01, 2002/03, 2006/07, 2007/08, 2008/09, 2010/11, 2012/13.

FA Cup 1989/90, 1993/94, 1995/96, 1998/99, 2003/04.

Football League Cup 1991/92, 2005/06, 2008/09, 2009/10.

FA Charity Shield/Community Shield 1990 (shared), 1993, 1994, 1996, 1997, 2003, 2007, 2008, 2010, 2011.

UEFA Champions League 1998/99, 2007/08 (runners-up 2008/09, 2010/11).

European Cup Winners' Cup 1990/91.
European Super Cup 1991.
Intercontinental Cup 1999.
FIFA Club World Cup 2008.

On top of all this, Ferguson achieved a plethora of individual honours, including a knighthood, all of which were won post-FA Cup Final in 1990.

Now, you might be thinking that this final chapter is a look back on the career of Sir Alex Ferguson at Manchester United and, while to a degree that does seem to be the case, the point is that if it wasn't for Lee Martin and his goal in that Wembley final, none of the last few pages could possibly have been achieved, such was the negativity surrounding the manager at the time. That goal was a real butterfly effect moment for both the club and the boss. In fact, you could even say it was for the fans as well. No one could have predicted the glittering future of the football club that followed the summer of 1990, particularly after the winter of discontent in 1989.

The banner that drapes across the mid-tier of the Sir Alex Ferguson Stand reads 'The Impossible Dream Made Possible' and highlights the 30-plus trophies Ferguson brought to Old Trafford. While Ferguson gave us success beyond our wildest dreams, Lee Martin should forever be etched in Manchester United folklore for kickstarting a dynasty at the club. Martin himself suffered with fitness and form after that cup final and went on to leave United in 1994 for Celtic, where a broken leg suffered within months of signing for the Glasgow giants signalled the start of a career decline before his retirement in 1998. But, like an avalanche, his goal and the winning of that trophy gave the club a momentum that kept on building with such force that eventually it peaked a decade later with an historic Treble.

It's a good job the board decided to stick with their manager. Imagine a parallel universe in which we lived through the other side of the time tunnel. Alex Ferguson is sacked after United lose the FA Cup Final to Crystal Palace on penalties and the club appoints Graham Taylor, who instantly falls out with Mark Hughes and Bryan Robson. Half of his old Watford team come through the door and the club struggle to find any form in any competition over the next 18 months. Attendances fall and there is huge disdain towards the club and the board. Taylor is then relieved of his duties and Ian Porterfield takes the reigns but is unable to save the club as they slip back into Division Two.

Makes you wonder, doesn't it? And if Colin Gibson had stayed fit, who knows what the dynamic of the team would have been moving forward. Luckily for us, Martin popped up at that back post and what followed were some of the most euphoric times you could possibly imagine. Thank you, Lee. Your goal gave me and millions of others the best years of our lives supporting this football club. Some finish, by the way.